THE ROYAL BEDSIDE BOOK

Also by Helen Cathcart:

THE QUEEN AND THE TURF
HER MAJESTY
SANDRINGHAM
THE QUEEN MOTHER
ROYAL LODGE, WINDSOR
PRINCESS ALEXANDRA
LORD SNOWDON
ETC. ETC.

Helen Cathcart

THE ROYAL BEDSIDE BOOK

W. H. ALLEN · LONDON · 1969

Printed and bound in Great Britain by The Garden City Press Ltd., Letchworth, Herts., for the publishers W. H. Allen & Co. Ltd., Essex Street, London WC2.
491 00133 9

Contents

Illustrations

Author's Note

I wish first to express my grateful appreciation to H.M. The Queen for her gracious permission to reproduce the photographs of her more personal household treasures which appear in these pages.

I am indebted to the secretariat of the State Library in Coburg for enabling me to locate and translate the London journal of the Duchess Augusta of Saxe-Coburg, Queen Victoria's grandmother, which here appears in English for the first time and may, I hope, be regarded as a sequel to an earlier journal, *In Napoleonic Days*, selected and translated by Princess Beatrice.

The archivists of the Public Record Office and the Ministry of Defence assisted materially in enabling me to unfold the story of the Boy Jones which, it appears, has not previously been told "in depth".

I am also most grateful to Dr Caldeira Coelho, of the Foreign Ministry of Portugal, for smoothing my enquiries into "The Other Prince Consort"—King Ferdinand of Portugal—and to Dr Cid de Oliviera, among others, for his hospitable assistance at Luso and Bussaco.

In my study of Princess Alice, mother of Prince Philip, the Duke of Edinburgh, I am particularly indebted to the Broadlands Archives and to members of the Royal Family of Greece and Denmark for incidental reference and correction. The vigilance of the archivists of Messrs. Coutts and Co. and the researchists of *Reader's Digest* and *Chatelaine* proved fruitful in enabling me to complete the chapters upon "The Queen's Mail" and "The Queen's Money". Mr

Harold A. Albert similarly first drew my attention to the amusing circumstances of Prince Philip's Debut and I again owe him a special debt for his unfailing patience in editorial assistance. My debt for help and information elsewhere must be mentioned if only to acknowledge my awareness of the patience, kindness and courtesy with which busy people permit my incursions into their time.

HELEN CATHCART

ROYAL YESTERDAYS

1 Queen Victoria's Grandmama Visits England

Queen Victoria never forgot her childhood impressions of her Saxe-Coburg grandmama's only visit to England in 1825. Her grandmother's own impressions, told in letters home from Claremont and Kensington Palace, are now with permission translated into English and published for the first time.

In the year 1757 a daughter was born to the Count and Countess Henry XXIV of Reuss-Ebersdorf and christened Augusta, perhaps a token of disappointment that she had not been born a boy. No fewer then fifty Counts of Reuss had ruled their tiny domain in unbroken succession for centuries, and the advent of a girl-child seemed of small significance. Yet the blue-eyed infant was destined to become the grandmother of both Queen Victoria and Prince Albert, and her influence still lingers in the House of Windsor in the twentieth century, six generations back in the ancestry of Queen Elizabeth II.

At twenty, Augusta of Reuss married the kind and gentle Prince Francis, who succeeded his father as Duke of Saxe-Coburg in 1800 when their family of four daughters and three sons were just growing up. Broken and impoverished by the Napoleonic wars, he died six years later and it was largely due to his widow's courage, resolution and unswerving family purpose that the Coburg destinies ascended to their zenith.

"In 1826, I think, my dear Grandmother, the Dowager Duchess of Saxe-Coburg, came to Claremont in the summer. I recollect the excitement and anxiety I was in, going down the great steps to meet her . . ." So wrote Queen Victoria in her private reminiscences of childhood. Her memory betrayed her, for the visit occurred in 1825. Imagine my excitement then, when delving into the records of that year in the State Library of Coburg, I chanced to discover her grandmama's own account of the event, chiefly to her eldest daughter, Sophia, Countess Mensdorff-Pouilly. Translating them page by page enchantingly revealed a vanished world, freshly seen by Grandmama with wit and worldly shrewdness.

The Duchess Augusta was then in her sixty-eighth year. Her youngest son, Leopold, still resided at Claremont as widower of the Princess Charlotte and six years were to pass before he became King of the Belgians, the "Uncle Leopold" of Queen Victoria's letters. Her youngest daughter, Victoire, had married King George IV's younger brother, the Duke of Kent, who died when their only child, Victoria, was but eight months old. Twice widowed, the Duchess of Kent had two children by her first marriage. Twenty-year-old Prince Charles escorted his grandmama to England when his sister Princess Feodora was seventeen and living in England, and his half-sister, little Victoria, was only six years old as she steals unforgettably into these charming letters. At Calais, the travellers were greeted by Prince Leopold's comptroller, Sir Henry Seton:

Claremont, 6 August, 1825

I have been here since half-past four on the twenty-ninth, my dear one, but have had little time to think, since all my scattered children wish to be informed that I arrived safely and happily. The sea-crossing, on a very imposing steamer, took only two hours and twenty minutes. Charles and the nannies felt miserable, but I, Sir Henry and the chambermaid kept well. Very soon the chalk cliffs of the English coast appeared, and then the dark gloomy castle of William the Conqueror, and as we entered the harbour we were greeted by a salute of cannon.

The good old Captain Hamilton led me to a carriage and I arrived, still a little dazed, at the very clean inn on the harbour, where Sir Henry and Charles had already ordered a very plentiful *déjeuner*. We were given two sentries . . . and like a dumb fish I made a curtsey to the officer.

Our departure was again accompanied by a gun-salute, and we sped through old Dover, which has new streets and darling little houses. We ladies travelled with Sir Henry in a coach belonging to Leopold, Charles in front; but the English stage-coaches, with their elegant red-uniformed postillions, look like carriages of the nobility. Seton had to name all the villages and every estate. Half-way to Canterbury, I went to sit beside Charles in order to see the surroundings better. The long drought has shrivelled up everything here as well!

We changed horses at Canterbury, and went to the ancient Cathedral where Henry II had Thomas à Becket murdered hundreds of years ago. They still point out the exact spot and the martyr's grave. The Cathedral, enormously big, is being repaired in pure Gothic style.

Near Faversham, the surroundings are beautiful; the trees lovelier, and with a richer foliage, than anywhere on the Continent. The country houses, the uniquely delightful villages, cannot be described; everywhere is not only neat but subtly elegant; an abundance of flowers! In one village, the pastor's residence was like something out of a novel. Sittingbourne, where we stayed overnight, was a so-called village; only two rows of houses, but how pretty they were!

I would have wished you here. At least ten stage-coaches and mails passed through, filled to capacity with people. It is not permitted to cram more than eighteen persons into them. As soon as they drive through a place, the conductor blows a sort of hunting-horn to prevent anyone from getting on. Here, all the horses are changed, and the odd items unpacked and packed again, which would have amused you very much. . . .

We left Sittingbourne at nine o'clock. The road is always good, and the neighbourhood beautiful, hilly with a lot of cornfields. Near the large, industrial town of Chatham, one sees the heavenly Thames which stretches out to the distant sea, filled with all sorts of ships, from three-masted ferryboats to the light barge and steam boats. This sight of the broad rough river alive with innumerable ships is unique! Then Rochester, and we had breakfast in Dartford, a pretty town. On our departure, the air seemed to glow and the dust was enough to suffocate one so, fearing a fainting fit, I joined Charles in his open chaise at the top of Shooter's Hill and had a look at the most beautiful view in the world.

Stretching out at our feet lay unending London, with its parks covered by a thin veil. The whole neighbourhood seems like a big park with gardens, and big and small country houses scattered around. Camberwell seems to be a part of London, since the rows of buildings are continuous, like the mail and stage-coaches. We changed horses again here and rode from country house to country house. One cannot think of anything more diversified or prettier; some are quite new and have been built on speculation.

The older ones either have fine gardens full of flowers—I saw in bloom the most lovely mallows I have ever set eyes on!—or large parks, in whose shade they stand. So many-sided, so delightful, all drawings of English country houses, lodges and cottages scarcely give one the right impression.

A kind of Gothic style is now fashionable, and very convenient, since one of these fantastic three- or eight-sided buildings can be placed anywhere. Such houses are really my passion; nothing can be nicer; doors and windows in Gothic style, the houses built in brown brick, and the windows, ramparts and pillars made from dazzling white stone. In addition, the colourful flower-garden or a verandah with climbing plants, even exotic ones. I felt as though intoxicated. . . .

Now I must make haste, since Pold (*Leopold*) is taking this letter to town with him. I don't have to tell you how warmly and affectionately he received me; he is so pleased to have his old Mother staying with him. Not far from Kingston, Victoire and Feodora came to meet us. The poor thing (*her daughter, Victoire, the widowed Duchess of Kent*) looks so ill and has lost so much weight that I had to force myself not to burst into tears. I am not going to attempt to describe her happiness at seeing me. Feodora is a most lovable girl, rather pretty, clever, amiable . . .

Little Mouse (*the future Queen Victoria*) is charming: her face is just like her father's, the same artful blue eyes, the same roguish expression when she laughs. She is big and strong as good health itself, friendly and cuddlesome—I would even say obliging—agile, poised, graceful in all her movements. We understand one another fairly well but are on the best of terms. Farewell, I simply must close. Such a rush quite robs me of my composure. Always yours.

Claremont, 10 August, 1825

My Dear, I want to begin my scrawl here. It is all too long since I heard from you, but that doesn't prevent me from writing. The air is doing me good. Lovely Claremont is situated in a warm and dry position, built in the Italian taste, sheltered by its giant trees. Since I can reach the terrace, and the fresh air, direct from my room, I naturally go for walks, as at the Rosenau . . . and I often get lost—what darling, shaded glades.

At my dear window, I sit writing at a tiny table, which I carried there myself, better than sitting at a comfortable desk, which stands in front of an equally comfortable chaise-longue. The view on to a lonely stretch of parkland is so lovely, with its groups of mighty fir trees. To the right, a wonderful cedar tree stands alone, to the left, there is a pond between the trees. Unfortunately, it rains every day for several hours—Oh, dear, it's thundering now!

Since I breakfast very early, as at home, I have long since taken my walk . . . and the most interesting thing is that with the telescope I can see Windsor Castle—so clearly that I can count the windows.

The building consists of a huge mass of towers and buildings, so that from a distance one has an impression of an old town rather than a castle. In the mornings, when the sun shines, there is a romantic light over the dark trees.

My friendly room has pale green wallpaper, on which hang pictures framed in gold. All over the house, the woodwork is painted in white and gold: chairs, armchairs, cushions, have a white groundwork. After nine o'clock, we all dine in the large dining-room, which has noisette wallpaper, gold-framed pictures, black chairs covered with red morocco. After breakfast, I read and write, and the Little One (*Victoria*) comes in for a moment, with her admirable governess (*Lehzen*) whom I like immensely. She is a lovable child, so vivacious and so friendly, and my conversation is improving daily.

I could speak quite well, if only I understood what the others were saying to me: unfortunately, once the chatter begins I find myself unable to think clearly. Sir Robert Gardiner, who was an equerry to Charlotte (*Princess of Wales, Leopold's dead wife*) takes indescribable pains, yet I understand no one less, because the poor dear man is a little affected.

With the Little One it is quite good. When I speak incorrectly, she says quite softly, "Grandmama must say . . ." and then tells me how it should be said. Such natural politeness and attentiveness as that child shows has never come my way before. . . .

Lady Gardiner is often my companion. She is certainly a dear, good woman who would be pretty if her complexion were not so highly coloured. Sir Robert is a little boring, though he has very good manners. Coffee is served in the library, an immensely large room so crowded with furniture that one can hardly move. . . . Three walls are taken up by bookshelves, the fourth by the fireplace and three large pictures: George III, Leopold and Charlotte. In the centre of the room are two sofas, far enough apart to allow two thin rosewood tables. Behind one table stands a piano, at which there is singing in the evenings. Feodora sings as well as her mother, and Leopold also sings with them.

Yesterday all the seats were occupied—the Cambridges were here. The Duke (*George IV's youngest brother*) is still a handsome man. Mrs. Paget (*another visitor*) is still pretty: here the country is ruled by the best teeth. The eldest Paget daughter is also not ugly, but frighteningly vivacious, such a lively Miss who wants to catch a man by her chatter. There is also Mr Horace Sim, who was a famous beau a few years ago, very big: his wife is a tall, slender, embarrassed brunette.

Before the meal, we sat, a little stiff, in the drawing-room, which has striped yellow silks and beautiful gilt furniture, and also old lacquered tables and cupboards, and a table of *porcelaine de Sevres*, white and gold. . . . The Pagets stayed till half-past nine; such a visit weighs heavily, particularly since the English women are so silent. Tomorrow I shall visit Victoire in town.

Kensington Palace, date illegible.

Bon jour, my dear. Victoire tells me that my letter leaves from town today at three o'clock, so I want to close it quickly and will only tell you that on several occasions I have already seen Princess Sophie-Mathilde of Gloucester, goodness and forthcomingness personified, not at all ugly at fifty years of age, has a very good figure. And yesterday the Duke of Sussex (*brother of George VI and the Duke of Kent*) who is shrewd and amusing, very polite, as all the brothers are when they want to be. He is very stout, dark like the late Kent, but not such a nice-looking face, though not ugly, more like the Mecklenburgs.

We were in Hampton Court, the immensely large palace begun under Cardinal Wolsey. It seemed to me, crossing the large hall, as if Queen Catherine and her Court and the beautiful Anne Boleyn would come down the broad winding stairway.

We were at Gainshill once, a very beautiful park, owned by old Lady Sudhampton. Then we went to Boxhill, situated on top of a hill where the view is superb. This Boxhill was covered with box trees which the present owner had felled for £10,000. He sold it in London as furniture timber. My goodness, how expensive everything is in this country! I am too poor, with my little bit of money, to buy all sorts of things.

Every afternoon excursions are made to the pretty environs. The country people are nice and friendly, their villages are darling little towns, with little cottages or country seats of the squires. On Sundays the inhabitants sit quite relaxed in front of their pretty houses, or in their gardens. Only the workmen wear peasant clothing.

Leopold has bought very important estates and three or four farms, and a large oak forest. The payment embarrasses him a little; but he is right in stating that "one must have something that one can call one's own", since Claremont belongs to the Crown. I have visited a cottage named Haywood by the little river Mole where Sir Robert Gardiner lives with his family. Nothing could be nicer or more cosy.

The little drawing-room which leads into the garden is furnished with the most sophisticated and yet simplest elegance. Spanish jasmine frames the front-door and gives fragrance to the rooms, and beautiful children, looking as if they were made of porcelain, embellish the whole. I would like to dig Haywood up for you and bring it to you.

Pold and Victoire wish to be remembered. Tell Fanny that in all the villages I see Miss Emma and poor Miss Taylor and good Miss Bates, with her obliging neighbour. (*Characters from Jane Austen*). With all my soul. . . .

Kensington Palace, 17 August, 1825

Today, on the birthday of my dear Victoire, I shall not write much. To be here, with her children, on her dear birthday, is something that at my age I had no longer counted on; and you, with your soft heart, will imagine how deeply moved I am.

Feodora woke her mother with her sweet voice and the Little One (*the future Queen Victoria*) scattered flowers around her. She already prepared yesterday, having dressed all her dolls in their Robes of State, with the help of Lehzen, who is her great love. Feodora, who takes after her mother in attentiveness and in her zeal to give pleasure, decorated the birthday table, before her mother was dressed, with a big ivy wreath and the most beautiful flowers. I put a coloured Neapolitan box on it; her daughters' bracelets with their portraits on. The Duke of Cambridge left a very lovely golden cross with turquoises. Spaeth (*the Duchess of Kent's companion*) gave a lace cap and Pold is going to bring a Parisian scarf. The Princesses (*Sophia and Mary, sisters of George IV*) will give a cross of balai rubies.

I left you at ten this morn to make an adorable trip on the Thames in a little boat belonging to the Admiralty. Victoire had ordered it and we sailed down the heavenly stream for four hours . . . under Westminster Bridge and Waterloo, the most beautiful in Europe, Blackfriars, the decorative iron one and finally under the big old London Bridge. Till then one sees only ordinary craft as on the Rhine, but beyond lie the big ships which sail to all parts of the world from the huge metropolis. . . .

We travelled into the basin which houses West Indian ships, two just being unloaded with coffee and sugar. I did not go into the shed because unfortunately there were big steps. The authorities gave Victoire the list of those items currently there:

148,563 baskets and crates of sugar.
433,638 bales of coffee, cocoa and cinnamon.
35,158 crates of rum and madeira wine.
14,021 blocks of mahogany.
21,663 blocks of stained wood.

When all sheds are filled to capacity—and Victoire only went into one—the value is rated at fifteen million pounds sterling. Doesn't that make you feel dizzy? Now I turn the page. . . .

Kensington is rather large, and has nice old houses, those along Hyde Park will soon be a part of London. The old Palace is a tiny bit sad, and not sufficiently bright, as there are windows only along one side of the rooms. The garden or, more precisely, park, since there are avenues and little woods of the most heavenly trees, is very lovely. On one side is a round piece of water, which seems to be surrounded by woods.

The large trees of Hyde Park shut out the view. I am very fond of them; they create a real atmosphere of being alone with nature until about mid-day, when all sorts of people take their walks, though not at all commonly dressed.

Every gate into the park has its own porter, and along the wall of the park by the palace sentry-box lies the road to Portsmouth. Every day 1500 Stage and Mail coaches leave London, the prettiest coaches, and even if there are only 300 here the noise seems to last all day and night.

Excuse du peu. When Victoire first lived here, all the good people, even the fashionable ones, went right up to the windows. Kent ordered, not without bother, that a small iron railing should be erected, about 40 paces from the lawn to the first avenue, and this barrier allows no one to enter its confine.

I have already had the experience of being frightened at night. I live practically at ground level and climb a little staircase to reach the garden; and in spite of watchmen who walk to and fro at night, and the keepers who lock the park, it is said that the woodland areas are not at all safe.

I must abruptly close, a messenger is taking my letter . . . I shall send you my diary.

12 August. We drove to London via Hyde Park and drove for three hours around the vast city. We saw the wonderful diorama, only two tableaux, Chartres Cathedral and the ruin of Holyrood Chapel in the moonlight. A masterpiece of optical artistry.

13 August. It rained the whole day! In the evening we visited the French Opera, where the glaring gaslight half-blinded me, and the large auditorium, crowded to bursting point, made me feel quite dizzy. The memory kept me awake that night.

14 August. I visited Leopold in his awe-inspiring but gloomy Marlborough House and accompanied him to the impressive Westminster Abbey. One cannot walk unmoved among the tombstones of the famous of the past 800 years, where friend and foe lie so peacefully side by side.... Though very tired, I still went to a dinner invitation to the Duke of Sussex, an enormous man who has innumerable little rooms. He seemed pleasant but spiritually odd ... and Antonia (*a lady in waiting*) tells me I made a mistake in the day!

16 August. Spent the morning with the best jeweller in London. The famous are in the habit of depositing their valuables. The wonderfully beautiful Vermeil silver service of the Duke of Northumberland was being cleaned: I have never seen such craftsmanship. Among the jewellery I shall mention only a solitaire worth £40,000. The value contained in two large rooms was close on two million.

Kensington Palace, 22 August

My dear, a little more.... We made a delightful trip by carriage to Hampstead, situated on a hill from which one can see the whole town as well as a wide stretch of countryside. In the light of evening, the town looks as if it is shrouded in the red smoke of a conflagration, and we continued via Highgate, and the newest and most beautiful part of the town, Regent Street, which reminded me of Petersburg.

Yesterday in the afternoon we drove over Battersea Bridge, behind the town, a delightful district, where there are meadows, hedges, lovely trees and nice little country houses, and returned over Vauxhall Bridge. Hundreds of boats carrying holidaymakers were sailing on the river.

On Sundays the parks are very pretty, John Bull and the fashionable world wander around in their coaches, but this is not the season, and so people say that No-one Is In London, only a hundred distinguished people are absent in a town of one and a half million people. But those who wish to appear distinguished do not in fact go for walks!

On Saturday I went to the Bazaar, as at home, but not nearly so well stocked. The cheap articles were ugly and the pretty things quite beyond my means. It is said that things are getting more expensive all the time.

Also we visited the Tower, most imposing, which housed the Kings until Henry VIII built the muddled palace of St James's. From there, to the lovely St Paul's Cathedral, which looks from the outside as if it were armed with chimneys! In the evening to the Haymarket Theatre. The actors are excellent, with my inadequate English still amusing—a pious host who insists on the rectitude of his household; a lady of easy virtue who arrives on horseback; a dissolute, divorced man and a very massive woman. The faces! Leopold laughed, in spite of Feodora.

I'm enjoying myself very much here, but the oppressive air chokes me, and I long for the fresh, clean air of Claremont. The London fog, which never allows the daylight to appear except for the odd hour, comes here when there is an east wind. Farewell, and always yours. . . .

Claremont, 12 September, 1825

I received your letter of the second, my dear, when I felt a very ill and miserable person, having a swollen face until the silly abscess on my tooth had abated. It is a pleasure to write to you, you poor, dear Good One, since you put such a high value on my silly scribble . . . You ask about Victoire. In the evenings, when she has applied a little rouge, she is still very pretty, her figure so pretty, and she dresses very well, and very simply. The Little One (*the future Queen Victoria*) is nothing less than a beauty, yet a darling clown. Her little face has a special expression of seriousness when she doesn't know you. Her posture is like her mother's, and when she enters a room, and greets you by inclining her head, according to the English custom, there is a staggering majesty.

She is incredibly precocious for her age (*six years*) and very comical, I have never seen a more alert and forthcoming child. She talks to everyone and thinks a lot about what has been said. Recently Miss Knight stayed here for a few days; she was one of the many attendants of poor Charlotte, and is old and dirty, but clever and well-read, and is even an authoress. The Little One, unasked, and with a shy little face, conversed with her.

When she speaks German, she is adorable. She will not do it with me, "Grandmama speaks English", but she does with the young ladies. Recently I went out with her, the wind blew my hat to one side. The Little One looked very seriously at Antonia and said, "Antonia, my grandmama's hat doesn't fit properly." In the evening, when she collects me for tea, she quickly runs to the maid and says, "You must extinguish the light."

Since one is six years old with impunity, there is often bargaining whilst going to bed. Then she blames her Sarah, accusing her of hurting her while washing her. In the morning, she sometimes does not want to get out of bed, preferring to tell all sorts of tales. Lehzen takes her gently from her bed, and sits her down on the thick carpet, where she has to put on her stockings.

One has to contain oneself not to burst out laughing, when she says in a tragic tone of voice, "Poor Vicky! She is an unhappy child! She just doesn't know which is the right stocking and which is the left! I am an unhappy child!"

You are probably in Dresden now, where I hope it is as warm as here, though not as damp. It is raining often now and the air never seems to get dry . . .

Such lively robins as they have here can be found nowhere else. One is sitting on the window-sill now and singing, having run around the room for quite a while previously, catching flies. The laurel bush is inhabited by blackbirds and a large number of other small creatures, not however as tame as the lovable robins. When the evening sun shines across the glimmering green meadow into the tall trees, then my little place by the window is truly delightful.

Without fear, rabbits and pheasants roam at leisure and even the swans from the lake.

I cannot tell you how much society upsets me. One evening in Kensington, there was the Duke of Sussex, his son, Colonel d'Este, pretty and conceited, Princess Sophie, Count Gersdorf (his mother is a Hopfgarten), Ambassador Count Ludolph, a boring diplomat, and his wife, a Greek woman from Constantinople, no longer young and with such a blasphemous tongue that she might have come from London.

She blames the poor Countess of Munster for falling every few months for another nasty child. She was supposed to come that night and then declined the invitation. "You see, she is again with child!" said the Countess Ludolph. I was quite taken aback.

Farewell, love, I have written too much.

Claremont, undated.

It is probably my heartfelt love for you, whose life is so closely interwoven with mine, that makes me so enjoy writing to you.

After the English breakfast, at which I sit and perspire, I go into the park. There are not many benches, but I have a walking-stick which converts into a stool, given to me by the Duke of Sussex, which is carried by my servant, and at any spot which I like it is spread out and stands firmly on four feet. (I shall have a similar one made for you.) I put my work-basket down beside me, and work or read if the spot is especially charming . . .

When the others have their *dejeuner fourchette* at two o'clock, I dine with Vicky. Since Pold always goes out hunting now, for grouse on the heath, I suggested eating with the Little One less punctually, for my stomach revolted. In the afternoons I go for a drive with Feodora or the Little One or one of the ladies. Here, I love to drive. Today we went through Esher, a most pretty little place adjacent to Leopold's park, then down a friendly path through meadows, across bridges over the little River Mole, and through Oatlands, which was owned by the Duke of York, who sold it. The park is sad-looking: there is much dark woodland.

Then under shady trees to pretty Walton and through Weybridge by the Thames, which is certainly deep, for coal-barges are carried on it. At Kingston, two hours farther on, the surroundings become quite delightful: one after another magnificent country seats belonging to celebrated Lords, in which one can always find a lovely avenue with flower gardens seen through high wrought-iron gates. Rather common are the seasonal roses round the doors of the neat little cottages, and they even clamber up most ordinary houses and flower in a most friendly way after there has been some rain.

The scenery by the river going towards Richmond is indescribably pretty. On the big heath and along the woods, however, one sees single straw-covered poor-looking huts, which one suspects shelter poachers and robbers. At Hampton Court it always seems to me I must catch a glimpse of Henry VIII or Elizabeth riding into the dark palace. At Bushy, where the Clarences live, the park is made up of all sorts of avenues, but the house is surrounded by a little garden which has a bored look about it.

Last week the Duke and Duchess of Gloucester were here. (*Princess Mary, sister of George IV, married her cousin, the Duke of Gloucester.*) She is very polite and the prettiest of the King's sisters. He is certainly polite and—a little stupid, not half-witted, but approaching it. At the same time, Lord Henry Fitzgerald and his family, who lived for a long time in Paris . . . most civil.

Too comical, I must tell you that Lord George Hill, a young officer in the Hussars, has just disturbed little Vicky with his whiskers. Moustaches are not customary here, but the Hussars abuse a privilege and Lord George has a face so overgrown with such a jet-black moustache and beard that one had to forgive the child for showing such fear in her eyes. The young man was most upset about it, and Lord Fitzgerald said with a bold look—just like my brother—"It's a great consolation for Milord if all the young ladies are alarmed by his moustaches like the Princess."

Claremont, undated.

My dear, You were ill with a chill again, you naughty thing? Yesterday everyone got wet here, I and Feodora in an open carriage, Victoire a little riding on horse-back, Mr Huskinson, Minister of the Board of Trade, and Mr Paget, who were hunting with

Leopold. Mr Paget, the brother of Lord Anglesey, is more mischievous and comical than a forty-year-old Englishman ought to be permitted to be, and agreeable in addition!

Leopold the other morning covered seventeen German miles to Portsmouth, in order to witness a battleship being launched, named *Princess Charlotte*, and he was back again by night-time. This sort of thing is not done in Germany!

Your friend, the sixty-four-year-old, is right in maintaining that there is nothing more enjoyable than travelling in and around London, though there is nothing more strenuous . . . I don't want to miss a single stage-coach, because I am so amused by all the people sitting in it. In town the gas lighting completely blinds me; it has a glare about it which is unbearable. I look into one of the fairy-like glittering boutiques, my head aches.

Claremont, 26 September, 1825

For the last time I am writing to you, you Dear, from the charming, homely Claremont. Like music, the days intermingled with one another, and the eight happy weeks I have spent here have evaporated, a beautiful dream, never to return. Oh if only the parting with Victoire and the dear Little One were over, and I were already sitting in Calais!

I find that a "last day" is just too horrible. Already for some days Victoire and I cannot look at each other without crying. I have just been to the garden again, have roamed once again the dear paths, it was so autumnal. On the big lake at the end of the *bosquet*, the wild ducks were screaming as if they wanted to come across the sea with me, everywhere the yellow leaves on the trees were fluttering . . .

Oh, how painful it all was! I felt the sad "for the last time" deep in my heart.

Calais, 28 September, 1825

So now I am in Calais, and would give much to be able to take off and fly to Mainz. I won't say a word about the parting. I haven't been able to sleep last night or the night before, I had such a headache from being so upset. Good old Leopold accompanied me here. I drove with him from Claremont to Dover, and if he had not been there would have cried the whole time.

Today at nine we crossed and again the journey took less than three hours, I was affected even less than the first time, the air was milder. General Wetherall, who was in the service of the late Kent, a dear old man, also accompanied us. No one except poor Antonia was ill. The crossing was rather nice. Farewell, my dear, my eyes hurt a little from the sea air. Write to me at Mainz, where I shall probably remain until the seventeenth.

Always yours

So end the charming letters of the Duchess Augusta, Queen Victoria's grandmama, on her only visit to England . . . letters laid away for the past 140 years and perhaps never read by English eyes till now.

2 Queen Victoria Recollects Her Childhood

Among the special treasures of the Royal Archives at Windsor Castle is a little manuscript book of reminiscences written in Queen Victoria's characteristic flowing hand . . . her intimate memories of her own childhood set down in later life by the Queen herself.

*For many years a valuable source-book to historians, Queen Victoria's "Reminiscences of early childhood" still magically touch the heart.**

The story opens in the year 1821 when little Princess Victoria was two years old and her uncle, George IV, was on the Throne. Her mother was already widowed. Her mother's favourite handsome younger brother Leopold, had married the King's daughter, Princess Charlotte, but she had died in childbirth and the thirty-year-old widower still lived at the mansion of Claremont in Surrey.

"My earliest recollections are connected with Kensington Palace (*wrote Queen Victoria*). I can remember crawling on a yellow carpet spread out for that purpose—and being told that if I cried and was naughty my Uncle Sussex (*the King's younger brother*) would hear me and punish me . . . for which reason I always screamed when I saw him!

I had a great horror also of Bishops on account of their wigs and aprons, but recollect this being partly got over in the case of the Bishop of Salisbury by his kneeling down and letting me play with his badge of the Order of the Garter.

Claremont remains as the brightest epoch of my otherwise rather melancholy childhood . . . to be under the roof of that beloved Uncle Leopold, to listen to some music in the hall when there were dinner-parties and to go and see dear old Louie, the former faithful Dresser of Princess Charlotte, who doted on the little Princess . . .

I used to ride a donkey given me by my Uncle, the Duke of York (*another brother of the King*) who was very kind to me. I remember him well—tall, rather large, very kind but extremely

* Newly edited by Helen Cathcart

shy. The last time I saw him was when he was very ill—and he had Punch and Judy in the garden for me.

Then we used to go frequently to Ramsgate in the summer, and I remember going there by steamer. Mama was very unwell. Dear Uncle Leopold went with us. To Tunbridge Wells we also went, living at a house called Mount Pleasant, now an hotel. Many pleasant days were spent here, and the return to Kensington in October or November was generally a day of tears.

I was brought up very simply. I never had a room to myself till I was nearly grown up and always slept in my mother's room till I came to the Throne. At Claremont, and in the small houses at the seaside, I sat and took my lessons in my governess's bedroom. I was not fond of learning as a little child, and baffled every attempt to teach me my letters up to five years old. Then I consented to learn them by their being written down before me.

I remember going to Carlton House when George IV lived there, as quite a little child before a dinner the King gave. My aunt, the Queen of Wurtemburg (*eldest daughter of George III*) came over in the year 1826, I think, and I recollect perfectly well seeing her drive through the park in a Cap and evening dress in the King's carriage, with red liveries and four horses, having dined early with the Duke of Sussex at Kensington.

She had adopted all the German fashions and spoke broken English. . . . She was very kind and good-humoured but very large and unwieldy.

In the year 1826, I think, George IV asked my mother, my sister and me down to Windsor for the first time. He had been on bad terms with my poor father when he died, and then took hardly any notice of the poor widow and little fatherless girl . . . When we arrived at Royal Lodge, the King took me by the hand, saying, "Give me your little paw".

He was large and gouty but with a wonderful dignity and charm of manner. He wore the wig which was so much worn in those days. Then he said that he would give me something for me to wear, and that was his picture set in diamonds, which was worn as an order to a blue ribbon on the left shoulder. I was very proud of this. . . .

Lady Maria Conyngham and Lord Graves were desired to take me on a drive to amuse me. I went with them and Baroness Lehzen (my governess) in a pony carriage, with four grey ponies (like my own) and was driven about the park and taken to Sandpit Gate, where the King had a menagerie, with wapitis, gazelles, chamois, etc.

Then we went the next day to Virginia Water, and met the King in his phaeton in which he was driving the Duchess of Gloucester . . . and he said "Pop her in", and I was lifted in and placed between him and Aunt Gloucester, who held me round the waist. (Mama was much frightened.)

I was greatly pleased, and remember that I looked with great respect at the scarlet liveries. . . . We drove around the nicest part of Virginia Water and stopped at the Fishing Temple. Here was a large barge, and everyone went on board and fished, while a band played in another.

There were numbers of great people there. The King paid great attention to my sister (*Princess Feodora*) and some people fancied he might marry her! ! She was very lovely then—about eighteen—and had charming manners, about which the King was extremely particular. I afterwards went with Baroness Lehzen and Lady Maria to the Page Whiting's cottage. Whiting had been at one time in my father's service, and here I had some fruit and amused myself by cramming one of Whiting's children, a little girl, with peaches . . .

After dinner I came to hear the band play in the conservatory, which was lit up by coloured lamps, the King, Royal Family, etc. sitting in a corner of the large saloon.

On the second visit the following year in summer, there was a great encampment of tents, which were quite like a house, made into different compartments. It rained dreadfully on this occasion, I well remember.

We lived in a very simple plain manner (*at Kensington*). Breakfast was at half-past eight, luncheon at half-past one, dinner at seven—to which I came generally when it was no large dinner party—eating my bread and milk out of a small silver basin. Tea was only allowed as a great treat in later years.

In 1826 (I think)* my dear grandmother, the dowager Duchess of Saxe-Coburg, came to Claremont in the summer. Mama and my sister went part of the way to meet her, and Uncle Leopold, I think, had been to fetch her as far as Dover. I recollect the excitement and anxiety I was in, at this event, going down the great flight of steps to meet her when she got out of her carriage, and hearing her say, when she sat down in her room, and fixed her fine clear blue eyes on her little grand-daughter, "A fine child!"

She was very clever and adored by her children but especially by her sons. She was a good deal bent and walked with a stick, and frequently with her hands on her back. She took long drives in an open carriage, and I was frequently sent out with her, which I am sorry to confess I did not like. . . .

She was excessively kind to children, but could not bear naughty ones. I shall never forget her coming into the room when I had been crying and naughty at my lessons—coming from the next room but one, where she had been with Mama—and scolding me severely, which had a very salutary effect.

She dined early in the afternoon and Uncle Leopold asked many of the neighbours and others to dinner to meet her. My brother, Prince Leiningen, came over with her, and was at that time paying his court to one of her ladies, Countess Klebelsberg, whom he afterwards married—against the wish of his grandmother and mother, but which was afterwards quite made up. (*Here the Queen's memory perhaps slipped. The marriage was an unhappy one, and Prince Leiningen and the Countess were subsequently divorced.*)

In November my grandmother left, taking my sister back to Coburg. I was very ill at that time, of dysentery, which illness increased to an alarming degree. Many children died of it in the village of Esher. The doctor lost his head, having lost his own child from it, and almost every doctor in London was away. Mr Blagden (*a physician*) came down and showed much energy. I recovered and well remember being very cross and screaming dreadfully at having for a time to wear flannel next to my skin.

Up to my fifth year I had been very much indulged by everyone, and set pretty well ALL at defiance. Old Baroness de Spath, the

* In reality, 1825

The Duchess Augusta of Saxe-Coburg-Saalfeld.
(See QUEEN VICTORIA'S GRANDMAMA VISITS ENGLAND)

Prince Ferdinand of Saxe-Coburg & Portugal at the age of twenty-one.
(See THE OTHER PRINCE CONSORT)

devoted lady in waiting of my mother, my nurse Mrs Brock, dear old Mrs Louis—all worshipped the poor little fatherless child whose future then was still very uncertain (*the Queen is here speaking of her position in the succession*)—my uncle the Duke of Clarence's poor little child being alive, and the Duchess of Clarence had one or two others later.

(*Victoria's uncle, the Duke of Clarence, succeeded as King William IV, and it was on his death that Victoria became Queen.*)

At five years old, Miss Lehzen (*later Baroness*) was placed about me, and though she was most kind, she was very firm and I had a proper respect for her. I was naturally very passionate, but always most contrite afterwards. I was taught from the first to beg my maid's pardon for any naughtiness or rudeness towards her: a feeling I have ever retained.

Everyone should own their fault in a kind way to anyone, be he or she the lowest, if one has been rude to or injured them by word or deed, especially those below you. People will readily forget an insult or an injury when others own their fault, and express sorrow or regret at what they have done. . . ."

At this point Queen Victoria laid down her pen. The scenes of her childhood had passed before her, irretrievable and bitter-sweet, and now she found herself alone at her desk in the evening light. "I stand so alone now," she sadly confided at about this time to her own private journal, "no near and dear one of my own age left. . . ."

3 The Other Prince Consort

The "Ifs" of royal history afford a fascinating field for speculation. Supposing Charles I had not been executed or George V had never married? Supposing Albert had outlived Queen Victoria? The imagination browses in the realm of might-have-been and yet the course of Victorian events once provided a real alternative . . . for there were TWO "beautiful and clever" Prince Consorts from Saxe-Coburg.

"I do *so* love him . . . he is so sensible, so natural, so unaffected and unsophisticated and so truly good." Thus the young Victoria, two months before her seventeenth birthday, confiding her impressions to her journal amid the festivities at Windsor Castle for the visit of her two young Saxe-Coburg cousins. It was the year of destiny before she came to the Throne, and the year when her Uncle Leopold in Belgium already brimmed with plans that one of his nephews *at least* should successfully marry a Queen.

"The separation will be dreadful for the two brothers," Victoria wrote pensively, reflecting repeatedly on the contrast between the two young men, "both very dear and charming." But the one was "a dear boy, extremely good, kind and gentle . . . his eyes are so beautiful and he has such a lively, clever expression . . . something *quite beautiful* in his expression when he speaks and smiles and he is *so* good".

And then the farewells were said, the carriages grated away down the drive and, back at Kensington Palace, Victoria snatched up her pen and wrote fervently of her "*beloved*" cousin to her "dearest Uncle": "All, all is over now . . . I cannot tell you how sorry I was to see him go, for I love him dearly. He is so truly excellent, kind and good . . . I may venture to say that no one has his prosperity and happiness more at heart than I have. I doubt not that with good counsel, and prudence, he will do very well." And now suddenly the placid pool of reverie is shattered by the heron's beak of reality, for we have been dreaming of Victoria and Albert—and in March,

1836, Victoria was writing of her cousin, Prince Ferdinand of Saxe-Coburg, so superior to his younger brother, Augustus, as Victoria said, "in various ways".

It was May, 1836, before Victoria could write of the pair whom we all know rather better, "At a quarter to two we went down into the Hall, to receive my Uncle Ernest, Duke of Saxe-Coburg-Gotha, and my cousins, Ernest and Albert, his sons. Ernest is as tall as Ferdinand and Augustus . . . Albert, who is just as tall as Ernest but stouter, is extremely handsome; his hair is about the same colour as mine; his eyes are large and blue, and he has a beautiful nose and a very sweet mouth . . ." The rushing stream of events has seldom divided so fittingly into alternative courses. One is tempted to wonder—idly, perhaps—what the tempo of the nineteenth century might have been if Queen Victoria had never been born or how the history of the Victorian age might have differed if Prince Albert had not so sharply severed the century into two on his death-bed. And for once true events provide a parallel, as in a mirror, for Uncle Leopold's aspirations had focused upon two sets of his Saxe-Coburg nephews. There were to be two reigning Queens and two Prince Consorts; and in this strange counterpart it was the Queen who died and her consort who survived her for long years as a widower.

But perhaps we should follow the parallel stream to its source. One must return then to Coburg, with its gabled red roofs and steeples and echoing cobbles, where lived Victoria's grandmama, the strong-willed devout Duchess Augusta, who so successfully pushed the ducal House of Coburg into international prominence chiefly by stage-managing a series of brilliant marriages for her children. Her youngest daughter, Victoire, widowed in her mid-twenties, espoused as her second husband the rubicund Duke of Kent and became the mother of Queen Victoria. Her youngest son, Leopold, was similarly widowed in his mid-twenties after marrying Princess Charlotte of Wales and thus became Queen Victoria's uncle and her cousin by marriage. Her second son, Ferdinand, married the only child and heiress of Prince Kohary, the rich and powerful chancellor of Hungary.

The Duchess Augusta read with deep satisfaction that the nineteen-year-old bride had been covered with jewels at the altar and "looked like a rosebud". Visiting Ferdinand's home in the Vienna Woods three years later, Augusta doted on her two grandsons, Ferdy and Gusti (Ferdinand and Augustus), "sweet children . . . fair-haired little boys", as she noted in her diary. And to Ferdinand *pere*, the Duchess Augusta was bursting with news of two of her other grandsons. Her own eldest son, the Duke Ernest of Saxe-Coburg, had also given his name, Ernest, to his own first-born the year before, and now the infant Ernest also had a baby brother, "a very pretty child," Augusta once again noted. "He is to be given the old Saxon name of Albert."

The stage was thus set for the two sets of cousins, Ferdinand and Gusti, Ernest and Albert, and within a year all were taking their nursery meals together in a cool and lofty room of the Rosenau. The Duchess Augusta presently pretended that she could scarcely distinguish between the cousins, alike as four peas when they combined to sing glees as a quartet at one of her birthday celebrations. Growing into their teens, all four were in fact counters in the constant lottery of matchmaking presided over by Augusta and her beloved Leopold.

The play became intense when Leopold accepted the throne of Belgium and took as his own second wife the delightful Princess Louise of Orleans, daughter of Louis Philippe, King of the French. The prospect opened for Leopold, in the extraordinary hotch-potch of royal marital relationships, that the brother of Louise might marry Queen Maria da Gloria, the girl Queen-Regnant of Portugal, and so establish a promising Belgo-Portuguese alliance. But this was not to be and instead, with the speed of melodrama, Leopold was treated to the spectacle of Queen Maria marrying—at sixteen—a man nine years her senior who almost immediately caught pneumonia and died, leaving his child-wife a widow within three months of the wedding.

"It is really quite dreadful," the young Victoria entered in her journal, striking the first note of tragedy in her life-long jottings that were to teem with family bereavement, "the poor young Queen is left a widow at the early age of sixteen!" Victoria knew

Maria well. They had first met at a children's ball given by George IV when Maria had fallen down and hurt her face, leaving the floor in frightened tears, while little Victoria danced on with undiminished confidence.

"We have known each other since our eighth year. There is only a month's difference in age between us," Victoria was eventually to write, when the time came to mention that the sixteen-year-old Queen was engaged to her cousin Ferdinand. "She is far from plain, too; she has an exquisite complexion, a good nose and fine hair. I hear that Ferdinand is full of good and excellent qualities." But this was before Ferdinand and Augustus came to England en route to Portugal and the impressionable Princess Victoria could see for herself how very "unaffected, distinguished, handsome, good and clever" Ferdinand trully was. "Ferdinand leaves behind him here a most favourable impression on all parties . . ." she elaborated to Uncle Leopold. "I have even heard from some great Tories themselves that there was a great feeling for him in this country."

Could events have been any different? Could Victoria have married Ferdinand? There was room for matrimonial manoeuvre in Uncle Leopold's choice of a route to Portugal via England for the intending bridegroom. Leopold was more anxious to further the interests of his close and well-to-do brother, Ferdinand *pere*, than of his obtuse and eldest brother, Ernest, Duke of Saxe-Coburg. Besides, Leopold had only recently gone to great lengths to ensure that Ernest could take up the vacant throne of Greece and the candidate had procrastinated at such length with the politicians that negotiations fell through. In priorities, the boys, Ernest and Albert, came second best. There is every indication that Leopold earnestly commended his nephews, Ferdinand and Gusti, to the youthful Victoria and especially Gusti.

As if obeying instructions, early in that 1836 visit with their father, Augustus sat near Victoria after dinner but, compared with Ferdinand, she found him "extremely quiet and silent". The next morning found him seated next to Victoria at breakfest in the absence of Ferdinand whom, it must be said, habitually stayed late in bed. Under grown-up prompting, it was Augustus who went up to Victoria's sitting-room and moved about, as she steadfastly noted, "looking at things" or "reading the newspapers, never in the way". He was scarcely a year her senior and, under Victoria's hour-by-hour account, it becomes evident that the two youngsters were flung together as frequently as the adults could arrange.

"Went downstairs to see some paintings done by a Mr Cowen," Victoria narrates. "Augustus came in also and looked at them for a moment. Came up to my room and dearest Uncle Ferdinand (*pere*) came up to see me for a few minutes and then went down again. Augustus came up and stayed a little, while I was writing my letters and then went down. At twenty-five minutes to four dear good Augustus came up and sat in my room, looking at annuals till four. He assisted me in sealing my letters and we both made a mess, and he burnt a cover in sealing it for me, dear boy, which made us both laugh. He went down for five minutes, came up again and Uncle, after staying a few minutes, fetched him away."

All in all, Gusti must have been a disappointment to his family. But Victoria reports with a touch of triumph that they went driving out, "Ferdinand and I on the back seat", and of talking a good deal with Ferdinand and liking him "*more* and *more*". When the brothers departed, it was Ferdinand who vividly lingered in her thoughts, so much so that she sat down to her sketching pad and drew his portrait from memory, his splendid profile, his crisp curly hair, his manly chest and handsome uniform. A testimony to an emotion, the drawing still exists at Windsor.

The obdurate fact remained that the subject of Victoria's admiration was affianced to another, although promises could perhaps have been curtailed and negotiations explained away had she felt prompted to pour out her heart to Uncle Leopold as fully as she was soon to do over Albert three months later. The articles for the Portuguese alliance had been signed in Coburg in December but some delay ensued before they were ratified in Lisbon. Both sides were playing for time on technicalities. A so-called proxy wedding in Coburg on January 1st was scarcely legal nor seemly, for only a tight-trousered Portuguese diplomat, Count Lavradio, stood in for the bride.

For a few hours of adolescent emotion at Windsor, at all events, the fates hesitated . . . until all was lost. If Ferdinand still seemed reluctant to marry a plump young woman whom he had never seen, his qualms were overcome. He was to receive from the Portuguese treasury an allowance of £9,000 a year, to be doubled on the birth of a son, with bonus payments for subsequent children, and he renounced all claims to his Saxe-Coburg and Hungarian titles but was forthwith to be dubbed Prince Consort.

Uncle Leopold, in fact, prepared for him an elaborate treatise on kingship, headed *Directions and Advices*, and his secretarial right-hand, Dr Stockmar, ensured that Victoria had a duplicate copy to help prepare her mind for her own approaching duties and the role of her own future husband. Her governess, Lehzen, prompted her to read it out aloud after Ferdinand's departure and heed all the "important and sage advice" it contained. "Uncle advises him to listen (at the Queen's Council) and not to give his opinion until he has become acquainted with the characters of the persons in the Council," the willing pupil noted. "Dear Uncle Leopold is a model for every Sovereign". She may have first found cause to moderate her opinion within a few months on learning that Portugal was engulfed in revolution.

Prince Albert of course arrived in England for his wedding to face cheering crowds at Dover, Canterbury and in London. Prince Ferdinand disembarked from a British warship in Lisbon under the stony glare of thousands who watched his carriage pass in gloomy silence. Married only the day after this cool reception, he learned during his brief honeymoon that some of his personal *biedermeier* furniture from Vienna had been unpacked at the docks and burned by an angry mob. His young Queen is said to have fallen in love with him at first sight: his tall slim figure, his reddish hair, his wide blue eyes. But Maria herself instantly caused trouble by creating him commander-in-chief of the Portuguese army, and tactlessly bestowed the jewelled baton upon him in the very week when bread riots occurred in Oporto.

Prince Albert was not offered a similar prize until he had been married ten years and, profiting by Ferdinand's mistake, he prudently refused. Prince Ferdinand however made matters worse by immediately issuing a first order of the day, promising severe discipline and condign punishment for insubordination, in terms that made Army veterans flush with anger.

He had begun as he meant to continue, imperiously. Albert at first was not permitted to choose the gentlemen of his own Household. Ferdinand flatly threatened to pack his bags and return home if he could not dismiss the camarilla or private council of elderly ladies who formed a government hedge around his Queen. He relied on closer confidential advisers: Father Marcos, the Queen's chaplain, Dietz, his old Coburg tutor and Dr van de Weyer from Brussels. The first was a jovial monk who delighted the young couple with practical jokes. Dietz considered a girl of seventeen and a boy of nineteen of adequate age to govern a nation, and van de Weyer, one of Uncle Leopold's most experienced counsellors, encouraged the Prince vigorously to resist the smallest encroachment on his authority.

Ferdinand had a flamboyance and dash quite lacking in Albert's personality. He rode in the great annual steeplechase at Campo Grande and amazed the Portuguese by his daring fences. When revolution befell, he rode out at once to put himself at the head of his troops, only to find that officers and men had deserted the barracks and that he had no alternative but to bow to constitutional reform. Two months later, when the new system was upset by yet another insurrection, and the Queen's guard attempted to leave her pink oblong Palace of the Necessidades on the hills above Lisbon, the Consort recalled them to order, pursuing them sword in hand.

One is put in mind of the fiery though ineffectual courage of King Constantine of Greece in 1968. From 1836 to 1853 the politics of Portugal were no less complex, with the veering fortunes, triumphs and blunders of four political parties feverishly causing fourteen revolutions in fourteen years. Maria da Gloria was at one time urged to flee, despite her husband's vehement reassurances, and a force of rescuing English marines were actually landed. But Uncle Leopold prudently cautioned against extreme measures. "In ten years' time the King and Queen of Portugal will still be young sovereigns, and what they will obtain spontaneously from the country by the force of circumstance will be much more substantial."

Leopold was right, and the Royal Family survived each successive turmoil. In their second year of marriage Maria da Gloria presented her husband with a son, and another boy was born the following year. "If Albert is like Ferdinand, you should enjoy perfect happiness," Maria felicitated Queen Victoria, with a significance probably lost upon that young innocent. With the succession ensured, Ferdinand was also given the rank of King-Consort, a title which did not prevent stones being hurled at his new Majesty or his coachman from being scratched by an errant bullet. Out riding in his capital, the King would nevertheless leap his horse at a post or railing in sheer high spirits; and his gallantry, calm and good works gradually raised him to a firm popularity among his people.

Albert's elder brother, Prince Ernest, paid him a visit and reported home that Lisbon had Ferdinand to thank for public sanitation, a better police-force and improved and profitable agriculture. "The arrangement in the palace itself, such as table, cellar, service, are in good order and are on exactly on the same scale as the Saxon court," he wrote. "The cooking is particularly good, as it bears a great resemblance to our beloved household fare; I have already been surprised to see dumplings."

Ernest was taken to see his host's new castle of Pena on the wooded heights above Cintra, and gasped at discovering a medieval German dream, coming to life midway up a mountain under the toiling effort of an army of masons. Albert's enthusiasm in building Balmoral saw its counterpart in Ferdinand's passion for the improvement of Pena, where the raising of Gothic turrets, minarets, Manueline patios and every species of architectural fantasy went on regardless of cost for ten years. More than eight million francs were squandered before Ferdinand began furnishing, a regal extravagance evidently underwritten by his expectations from the rich Kohary estates in Hungary. Bedsteads enmeshed in coiling inlay, colossal sofas in the Gothic style, zebrawood dining suites and florid pieces that now portray the worst furnishing excesses of the nineteenth-century were shipped from London, Paris and Vienna.

Ferdinand's special pride was a salon in which chairs, tables, escritoires, everything, had been made of deer antlers and, in the eyes of its inhabitants, Pena was soon regarded as a store of choice furniture. Amid the bric-à-brac in the Queen's room were three chairs "of different patterns, but most commodious", the Queen's chair, the King's chair and the Marshal's chair. The latter was reserved for Marshal Saldanha, strongest of the would-be military dictators who held the reins of power from time to time, and whom the royal couple tamed by encouraging to spend his evenings with them, indulging in games of Truth or Consequences. In the morning Ministers would come with documents, and one diplomatic visitor gives us a picture of Ferdinand drastically in command.

"The Queen receives no one alone, but every one comes to Ferdinand, who listens to them, arranges their affairs for them, and then only admits them to kiss the Queen's hand. When the person enters the drawing-room, Ferdinand always precedes him and usually kisses her hand first...." Another contemporary record provides the domestic picture after tea, the Queen taking up her embroidery, the King "occupying himself in works of art, such as sculpture of ivory, engraving and drawing, conversation being of a friendly and general nature". Billiard-tables were installed. Despite the responsibilities he took up, Ferdinand was not to work himself to death like Albert. And it was the dark-eyed Queen Maria who died, on 15 November, 1853, in childbirth with her baby. She had borne eleven children in sixteen years, twice at the risk of her life, and doctors asserted that she was exhausted with child-bearing.

Preoccupied by the perils of war between Turkey and Russia, the death of her sister Sovereign did not unduly perturb Queen Victoria. Eight of Maria da Gloria's children had survived her: the two eldest Dom Pedro and Dom Louis, being aged sixteen and fifteen respectively. The elder was immediately proclaimed King Pedro V and King Ferdinand simultaneously declared Regent. At Windsor Castle, the accession of Pedro was recorded with no hint that his fate would ring like a death-knell on another November day eight years hence. Like Victoria and Albert, Ferdinand and Maria had often anxiously discussed the education of their children and agreed that they should travel as much as possible. While their father ruled but did not reign, the two boys accordingly set off on a grand tour of the courts of England, Belgium, Holland, Austria and Prussia. In 1855 they visited Italy, Switzerland and France and they were at the opening of the Great Exhibition in Paris that year which owed so much to Prince Albert's successful 1851 effort in London.

The Regency is sometimes described as "history without event". Portugal had not for years enjoyed such stability of government. Ferdinand's most striking gesture was to set free all the African slaves of the royal estates, signalising the freedom that he was himself to enjoy in the near future. When Pedro took over the active duties of kingship, at the age of eighteen, he similarly won over public opinion by helping to abolish capital punishment. Serious-minded dutiful Pedro was Queen Victoria's favourite of Europe's royal younger generation. "He is out and out *the* most distinguished young Prince there is," she had written, in discussing potential matrimonial alliances with Uncle Leopold. The puritan strain that the young King shared with Prince Albert became evident in his refusal to contemplate marriage until he had turned at least twenty-one.

But Ferdinand at forty was a merry widower. He had not stirred out of the kingdom for twenty years and had ripened under the southern sun into an affable, romantic figure. The sighs he aroused in feminine hearts is obvious by the glamorous impression he made upon one of his private visitors to the mist-girt heights of Pena, "a tall, well-formed man, clad in a jacket and green velvet breeches, high riding-boots, and a black broad-brimmed hat—absolutely the outline of one of Vandyck's characters; the eyes dark, the glance mild, the beard and moustache red . . ."

In his odd position as the masculine equivalent of a dowager Queen, Ferdinand would extend his hand to be kissed. His original unpopularity long since forgotten, he adored strolling among the people of Lisbon, over the mosaic pavements of his devising, watching hats flicker off at his approach and acknowledging each courtesy with a bow and a smile. He enjoyed walking unannounced into a workship, to install himself on a stool, light a cigar and watch the men at work, carpenters, furniture-makers, picture-framers, craftsmen of every kind. Paying for his entertainment with a handful of silver distributed to everyone in sight, age had nevertheless taught him not to appear extravagant. He roved through antique shops, but when pressed to make too costly a purchase—a picture, a collection of coins, a rare piece of jewellery—he exclaimed with a comic melancholy, "Alas, I have no money!" and would pull out his pocket-linings in proof.

Perhaps he also acquired interests of a more fleeting, warmer nature, but his early indiscretions as a widower were, in fact, discreet, although they evidently became known to Uncle Leopold. "I even went so far as to say that the beauty of the Levantine women was known to be very great", King Leopold was to write, listing the inducements by which he unsuccessfully tried to persuade his nephew to accept the throne of Greece. But the public knew only that Ferdinand took pity on caged animals, created the Lisbon "model zoological gardens" and tirelessly supported the arts. He was a painter and sculptor himself of more than average amateur status. He enthused about do-it-yourself carpentry, learned to paint on porcelain and, as one of his friends said admiringly, "might give lessons to many a locksmith."

There was time now to travel again and, outside his own frontiers, Ferdinand felt more at liberty to ransack the art shops and salesrooms, demonstrating the depth of his purse for the treasures he discreetly bestowed not on his own but on his son's palace. His most notable acquisition for Pedro, however, was the Princess Stephanie of Hohenzollern-Sigmaringen, whom he discovered while visiting the Princess Royal, Victoria's daughter, at Potsdam. Queen Victoria watched the courtship with interest, complained that Pedro was taking too long to propose and found it very odd indeed "to marry without a husband" when Stephanie was married to Pedro by proxy in a ceremony in Berlin.

"Poor Pedro, what a treasure he gets!" wrote the Queen. Stephanie paid a visit to Windsor on her way to Portugal and Victoria found her enchanting. And sadly, within a year, in July, 1859, her radiant delight in "the dear child" turned to the shocked disbelief of grief, for the young and lovely Queen Stephanie was dead. "Married at the same age as ourselves, the same difference between their ages as between ours . . . and now all gone, crushed, shipwrecked!" moaned the Queen, gazing incredulously at the telegram. Thus was yet another link forged in the chain of matching circumstances between Ferdinand and Albert, the dark thread finally broken by the Prince Consort's death.

On 9 November, 1861, two of Pedro's younger brothers, Joao and Louis, were in England when news reached the Queen that a third brother, Ferdinand, had died at fifteen of typhoid. Within four days of this shock, when the two brothers had only just embarked for home, Victoria and Albert heard with horror the incredible news that King Pedro had also died, and their thoughts flew to cousin Ferdinand. "Too awful," the Queen repined. "He who was so proud of his five sons to have two swept away." Moreover, it had been only a month since her good faithful servant, John Brown, had been speaking of losing three brothers within a week. The coincidence struck the Queen as though it had been "a sort of strange presentiment".

It was indeed stranger, darker, than anything she could suppose. In Portugal, while the new king, Louis, was tossing on the Bay of Biscay, Ferdinand for the second time took the oaths of a Regency. On Friday, 13 December, his two sons disembarked and plump twenty-three-year-old Louis began his kingship. At Windsor, Prince Albert died on 14 December, and, a week later, no one near the Queen could tell her that young Joao's days were also numbered. While the fever raged, a deputation of the Portuguese cabinet begged Ferdinand and the new King to quit the palace in order to save their own lives, the doctors insisting that this was the only prudent course and suggesting they should take refuge in the country house of Caixas. The King and his father hesitated to leave, but the emotion of the people was at breaking point after the sequence of royal deaths, and Ferdinand and Louis's reluctance was overcome at the sight of thousands upon thousands of people waiting with lighted torches, at dead of night, to light the way.

In both royal families the return to normality began with a wedding: the marriage in England of Queen Victoria's second daughter, Alice, to Louis of Hesse and in Portugal with the marriage of young King Louis to Maria Pia, daughter of the King of Italy. The latter alliance was hailed as an important link between two southern kingdoms, and there were hopes that Ferdinand might heighten the southern entente by ascending the vacant throne of Greece. But he declined. "I feared from the beginning that Ferdinand would not accept," wrote Uncle Leopold to his nephew Ernest in Saxe-Coburg, and Leopold was probably aware that Ferdinand had the strongest of all motives for not leaving Portugal at that moment. The shadows of bereavement were being dispelled by a new shining star.

Her name was Elise Hensler, an opera singer whom Ferdinand first saw at the San Carlos Theatre in Lisbon, appearing in Verdi's *Un Ballo in Maschera*. He was charmed by her voice, her dark eyes, her youth. She was then in her mid-twenties and Ferdinand was approaching fifty. In answer to his eager enquiries, the impresario of the San Carlos arranged that she should sing at a royal reception. The King-father, as Ferdinand was sometimes known, heard that she was an American, trained in New York, and that her father was in the tailoring business in Boston. But in the course of the musical evening, Ferdinand discovered not only the charm and warmth of her personality but also the remarkable fact that her father had once been pianist in the orchestra of the little Coburg Theatre. Indeed, Ferdinand had perhaps heard him playing during visits to Coburg and certainly he was known to the Duke Ernest.

Like Queen Victoria on hearing of his family tragedy a year earlier, Ferdinand saw the design of fate in this coincidence. Lovers have been united by less, and Mlle. Elise soon had her established domestic role under his protection. Time passed and it became obvious that the King-father's affections were deepening to permanence. The people shrugged, content that he should have found happiness: the mortal sin would surely be forgiven. The aristocracy feigned ignorance. The Papal Nuncio in Lisbon felt it necessary to deliver a rebuke, though couched in terms no harsher or more explicit than was needful.

There are glimpses in royal correspondence and memoirs of Ferdinand strolling in his galleries and gardens, accompanied on one side by a pet parrot that followed him like a dog and on the other by Elise. Their common interest in music flowered into other shared enthusiasms, notably in planning a palace that they might build together at Bussaco, in one of the sunniest and healthiest climes of Portugal, and in building up an extraordinary and highly specialised library. As *The Annual Register* has it, King Ferdinand became "an ardent book collector, his especial delight being in collecting from every country in Europe books, pamphlets and prints of all descriptions which had been forbidden by the government or police; and in this way he accumulated a perfectly marvellous collection of the forbidden literature of Europe". The E and F (Elise and Ferdinand) affair, as it was sometimes known, blazed into acute international controversy however in 1869 when Ferdinand was offered the throne of Spain.

A revolution had deposed the Spanish Queen Regnant Isabella II and left that nation swinging in an abyss between republicanism and a monarchy. Public opinion veered towards the second alternative but especially favoured a kingship that might unite the whole Iberian peninsular and end the rivalries of centuries. It was suggested, in fact, that Ferdinand should marry again within the blood royal and thus found a fresh Spanish dynasty.

Clearly the argument between love and duty had never been more intense. Ferdinand temporised, laying down impossible conditions, notably that he must be elected by three-fourths of the Spanish parliament and that his enthronement should have the agreement of England and France. Instead of debating his terms, the Spanish politicians seemed about to concede them when Ferdinand decided that love and duty were not after all incompatible and made the issue more obvious by marrying Elise Hensler.

By order of none other than the Duke Ernest of Saxe-Coburg, the bride was immediately raised to the dignity and style of the Countess d'Edla. The wedding probably delighted Ferdinand's son, King Louis, and other members of the family, but not so Louis's strong-minded wife, Maria Pia, who left Portugal "for the benefit of her health" only five days later. Ferdinand added to his Spanish terms the dictate that the Countess d'Edla should be received on all save official engagements as his consort.

Even then the Spanish toyed with the idea that the crowns of

Portugal and Spain one day be united by naming King Louis as joint heir. Louis for his part, then put an end to the negotiations with the blunt declaration that he had been born a Portuguese and would die a Portuguese. The Spanish had to fall back on their former dynasty; Queen Maria Pia returned in softer mood from the spas of Italy, and the King-father and his countess began an idyllic new existence based upon the Castle of Pena, their plans at Bussaco and their frequent visits to Royat, Biarritz and other French watering places, chiefly for pleasure rather than health.

In allowing our thoughts to browse over the Ifs of history, one wonders whether Prince Albert would have perhaps accepted the throne of Greece had he survived as a widower? Would political antagonisms have sooner or later exiled him from England, leaving his son, Edward VII, to enjoy an untroubled, longer and happier reign? One can hardly imagine that Albert would have remarried or become anything but a confirmed misogynist (save perhaps his affection for his daughters). Yet Ferdinand, according to one of his contemporaries, used to cause astonishment by his enthusiastic admiration and demonstrative affection for the Countess d'Edla, especially among Frenchmen "who never speak of their wives, either to praise or blame them, in their absence".

When General and Mrs Ulysses Grant visited Lisbon just after their term in the White House, courtesy required the presidential couple to call upon Ferdinand and his lady at Pena, and Mrs Grant was in a fluster about the manner in which a virtuous American should meet a morganatic wife. She was spared any embarrassment. Offering her visitors tea, the Countess also served tea-cakes which, she explained, she had made herself, proof of such domestic good grace that the uncertain Mrs Grant was completely won over.

Even the arbitrary Maria Pia could recognise her stepmother's good qualities. Among the pinewoods of Bussaco was a hunting lodge where the family was happily reunited, and indeed for many years the Portuguese regarded their Royal Family as a model for all Europe. We see Ferdinand in autumnal serenity with his Elise, riding the forest trails with his grandson, Carlos, with no inkling that the young man's life would end in assassination in the unborn twentieth century. Or we watch him in the evening lamplight, rather more portly than of old, still affecting the casual flamboyance of a velvet smoking jacket, his beard and moustachios trimmed in the style of Napoleon III. The kissing of the hands of royalty had been abolished twenty years earlier by decree, but the King-father still absently extended jewelled fingers to the artists, musicians and architects whom he so often entertained.

The concerts, the conversations, the sessions in his billiard room all agreeably passed the hours. He planned a private billiard room so large that four groups could play at once but no space remained for it at Pena. Not an inch remained for the smallest turret nor was there an empty corner in the gardens for one more "statue or fountain, gazebo or summerhouse". He applied himself industriously to the plans for the palace at Bussaco which he never lived to see. The outer building, castellated and decked in sculptured garlands, should be embroidered in turn by a gallery with twelve archways in the wedding-cake Gothic known in Portugal as Manueline. For summer days there should be a roofed terrace like a rotunda opening on to the garden. For State festivities a regiment on gala parade should be able to descend the main staircase. Not a stone was laid at Bussaco in his lifetime. But when the building of Bussaco began in 1900 fresh architectural plans were drawn up for the new era, and discarded in favour of Ferdinand's.

Drawing and music remained his delight. Almost to the end he still occupied his box at the Opera, though a grille was placed to hide the disfigurements of time and sickness from the audience. He died on 15 December, 1885 twenty-four years and twenty-four hours after the death of his cousin Albert.

Occupied with her own memories, it is not known whether Queen Victoria noted the occasion or felt a tremor of the evanescent alternatives that had passed her by.

4 Royal Gossip—Old Style

Lavender and printer's ink seldom mix . . . except in the royal gossip columns of yesterday, pasted into a Court scrapbook when Victoria was Queen.

An Eccentric Suitor

13 July, 1837

The Queen has for some time been much annoyed by the offensive personal attentions of one of her subjects, labouring under the delusion that he is one day destined to possess Her Majesty's hand. Every day, until Her Majesty's departure for the New Palace (Buckingham Palace), Mr —— has been a constant attendant at Kensington Palace, inquiring at the grand entrance the state of the Queen's health, and endeavouring to enter, for the purpose of writing his name in the visiting book. On one occasion he succeeded in doing so; but the moment it was discovered, a pen was drawn through the autograph.

On several days, since the death of His late Majesty (William IV), Mr —— has been actively engaged in assisting the workmen in weeding the piece of water in Kensington Gardens, which is opposite the windows of the apartments occupied by the Queen and the Duchess of Kent, in the hope of obtaining a sight of Her Majesty; and on each evening he has been waiting in his phaeton, in the Uxbridge Road, Her Majesty's carriage emerging from the private road in Kensington Gardens, when he would follow it in whichever direction it might proceed.

On last Monday evening, which was the last time the Queen took an airing up the Harrow Road, Her Majesty, after proceeding some distance, alighted, with her illustrious mother, for the purpose of walking for a few minutes; but scarcely had she done so, before Mr ——'s phaeton was observed advancing towards them, out of which he immediately sprang, with the intention of accosting them.

The Duchess of Kent, on perceiving him, instantly directed one of her pages to request Mr —— would not annoy Her Majesty, but again enter his phaeton and drive off. Mr —— refused to do so; when the Royal party immediately re-entered their carriage and returned to Kensington Palace, followed by the Queen's pertinacious admirer.

On Thursday last, when Her Majesty left Kensington Palace, Mr —— was noticed as being most vociferous in his demonstrations of loyalty on the Queen's entering her carriage; which she had no sooner done than he rushed out of the courtyard, and running at full speed down the avenue, and jumping into his phaeton, preceded the Royal *cortége* to the Palace at Pimlico.

Coronation Festivities

28 June, 1838

In the evening, the queen entertained a large dinner party at Buckingham Palace. The Duke of Wellington also gave a grand ball at Apsley House, in honour of the event of the day. By Her Majesty's command, all the theatres in London—the Italian Opera House excepted—and nearly all the other places of amusement were open in the evening gratuitously, and were filled with well behaved though rather motley audiences.

The confusion incidental to an indiscriminate free admission was avoided by furnishing tickets to applicants beforehand. The Olympic and Adelphi were only partially filled, in consequence of its not generally being known that they would be open, as their season had terminated. Vauxhall Gardens were closed, because the proprietors asked £750 for the night, which was regarded as an exorbitant sum, considering that the price of admission was only a shilling.

The inmates of the various prisons and workhouses were regaled with beef, pudding, and ale; the patients in the hospitals had suitable delicacies given to them; and the children at the charity schools were also feasted.

The Victoria pudding, made to commemorate the Coronation,

was composed as follows: 36 lb. suet, 16 lb. sugar, 52 lb. flour, 32 lb. raisins, 7 lb. Saltana ditto, 32 lb. currants, 4 lb. peel, 1 lb. spice, 1lb. salt, 8 lb. bread, 10 dozen eggs, 5 quarts of milk, 5 pints of brandy, peel of 12 lemons, 12 lb. pounded loaf sugar. The pudding weighed 2 cwts. when cooked, was as big round as a hogshead, and was partaken of by nearly 5,000 children.

Forcible Presentation of a Petition

Tuesday, 21 August, 1838

As Her Majesty was passing through the Triumphal Arch, at the entrance of the Green Park, on her way to Windsor, a man in the crowd threw a letter into the Royal carriage with such force as to strike the Queen in the face. Her Majesty did not appear at all alarmed, and the carriage passed on. A constable seized the man, and took him to the station house in Gardner's Lane. He was an Irishman, who had been in the army, and complained that he had somehow been defrauded of several hundred pounds.

Exhibition of Wild Animals on the Stage

24 January, 1839

In the evening, the Queen visited Drury Lane Theatre, this being the third visit since Her Majesty's return from Brighton. Mr Van Amburgh gave his exhibition of wild animals in the Royal presence; and after the performance of the evening was over, and the house empty, the Queen and her suite, attended by Mr Bunn, were conducted to the stage, where the process of feeding the beasts was exhibited by Mr Van Amburgh and his assistants.

Mr Van Amburgh had previously intimated to the Lord Chamberlain, that if Her Majesty pleased, he would enter the cage, and remain there while the beasts were feeding; but an intimation was given that the Queen preferred witnessing the natural fierceness of the beasts unaided by their tamer. Her Majesty was graciously pleased to express her satisfaction at these unprecedented exhibitions, and put a variety of questions to Mr Van Amburgh through the Lord Chamberlain.

Munificent Act of the Grand Duke Alexander

8 May, 1839

The Grand Duke Alexander of Russia visited the Tothill Fields House of Correction, and inspected every part of the prison most minutely, remaining nearly an hour and a half. When about to leave, His Imperial Highness requested the Governor to furnish him with the list of debtors in this prison, all of whom were confined for sums under £5. This was done and the various amounts due by each prisoner were paid by the Grand Duke, and the debtors instantly discharged, very much to their gratification and astonishment.

Royal Debts

11 October, 1839

The Queen having paid all the debts of her late father, the creditors, through Sir Henry Wheatley, presented an address to Her Majesty, expressing their gratitude for this act of Royal Justice and liberality.

An Insane Suitor

13 October, 1839

James Bryan, a native of Ayrshire, and a person of weak intellect, presented himself at Windsor Castle as a suitor for the hand of Her Majesty.

The Queen at the Opera

20 June, 1840

The Queen visited the Opera for the first time after the late atrocious attempt on Her Majesty's life, and the appearance of the Sovereign was the signal for a loyal demonstration of a very striking character. The audience rose, the National Anthem was sung with great enthusiasm, the assembly loudly cheering at the end of each verse, Her Majesty standing all the time, and graciously acknowledging the congratulations of the audience. When the singing of the Anthem was concluded, Prince Albert was called, and received three hearty cheers.

The Royal Nursery

December, 1840

Mrs Packer, a Scotswoman, was appointed wet nurse to the Princess Royal. The superintendence of the Royal Nursery was entrusted to Mrs Kempthorne, the widow of a former rector of St Michael's, Gloucester. 'Mrs Packer is a native of Edinburgh, where she was well known as Miss Augustus Gow. She is a daughter of the late Nathaniel Gow, of this city, and grand-daughter of the celebrated Neil Gow ("Famous Neil"). Mrs Packer studied music at the Royal Academy, London, with the view of becoming a public singer, in which character she appeared at several concerts.'

Narrow Escape of Prince Albert

9 February, 1841

While Prince Albert was skating in Buckingham Palace Gardens, the ice suddenly gave way, and he was immersed in deep water. His Royal Highness had to swim for two or three minutes before he was got out. The Queen was close beside the Prince when the accident occurred, and was the only person who had sufficient presence of mind to render her Royal Consort any material assistance. His Royal Highness, fortunately, sustained no injurious effects from his immersion.

Her Majesty's First Railway Journey

13 June, 1842

The Queen, in travelling from Windsor to London, for the first time made the journey by railway. Her Majesty was accompanied by Prince Albert and Count Mensdorff, and attended by a numerous suite. The intention of the Queen to travel to town by railway was only intimated to the authorities of the Great Western Railway at Paddington on the Saturday afternoon previous, and in consequence preparations on an extensive scale were ordered to be made for the transit of Her Majesty, which were carried into effect with the greatest secrecy. The journey from Slough to Paddington was performed in twenty-five minutes.

On the Beach at Walmer

12 November, 1842

Shortly after 10 a.m., the Queen and Prince Albert left Walmer Castle for the beach, and walked along the shore unattended for upwards of an hour. The wind blew with great violence, and Her Majesty appeared to be delighted with the scene, there being between 100 and 200 vessels in the Downs, driven in for shelter during the previous night's gale. During the Queen's walk, a poor man, who had in his possession a very curious dog, which had been saved a few weeks previously by the Deal boatmen from the wreck of a Russian timber ship, was accosted by Her Majesty, who desired to know what kind of animal it was. The poor fellow related its history, and appeared much gratified with the interest which the Queen took in the animal. In the evening, the Queen and Prince Albert drove through the town of Deal, and subsequently again walked on the beach.

Royal Bounty to Boatmen

14 November, 1842

The Queen was greatly interested in the fate of the crew of a galley which was observed from the coast to suddenly disappear. Her Majesty was much relieved on learning that the whole of the crew had been picked up by a passing steamer. The Queen sent to ascertain the circumstances of the Deal men who had lost their boat and gave £20 towards the purchase of a new one for them. The weather being again rough and wet, Her Majesty did not go out.

Visit to the Thames Tunnel

26 July, 1843

The Queen, Prince Albert, the Prince of Saxe-Coburg and Gotha, the Princess Clementine, and other distinguished persons paid a visit to the Thames Tunnel. In the progress of the illustrious party in the Royal barge down the river, they narrowly escaped being run down by the *Syren*, a Woolwich steamer. Flags were hoisted at the Tunnel works and from various other places in the vicinity, and a scene of great animation presented itself in all quarters.

From the shortness of the notice given of the intended visit of Royalty to this great undertaking, but few preparations could be made for the proper reception of the august visitors. Indeed, most of the directors were out of town; and even Sir Isambert Brunel, the engineer, under whose auspices the works were commenced and completed, was too far from town for a communication to reach him in time to be present. Having proceeded through the Tunnel and returned, Her Majesty was pleased to express her gratification at being enabled to witness the completion of the Tunnel, and her regret that Sir I. Brunel was not present. The arrangements, though hurried, were well carried out, and the Queen re-entered the Royal shallop amidst the loud and hearty cheers of thousands of spectators, the bells of the churches in the vicinity at the same time ringing out a merry peal.

First Excursion in The Royal Yacht

28 August, 1843

The Queen and Prince Albert left Windsor Castle at 7.35 a.m. and went by special train to Southampton. The station was hung with a profusion of flags of all nations, and was wreathed with flowers. Her Majesty then drove through the station to the pier. Throughout the whole line of route, the streets were decked with flags and banners, and the windows were filled with ladies, who greeted the arrival of the Queen and Prince Albert by the waving of handkerchiefs.

At the pier head, moored some five yards off, was the Royal yacht *Victoria and Albert*. As rain was falling at the time, and the landing stage was wet and dirty, the members of the Corporation, like so many Sir Walter Raleighs, stripped off their robes of office in a moment, from which those of the Mayor and Aldermen were selected (they being scarlet), and the pathway was covered for the

Sovereign's use; so that Queen Victoria, like Queen Elizabeth, walked comfortably and dry footed to her barge. Her Majesty appeared much gratified by this spontaneous act of attention, and was pleased to step so as to avoid the velvet collars of the robes of office.

Ojibeway Indians

20 December, 1843

A party of nine Ojibeway North American Indians were presented to the Queen and Prince Albert at Windsor Castle. The Chief made a speech, in which he described the loyalty of his tribe, and the great satisfaction he and his countrymen felt in beholding Her Majesty. The party then performed several of their national dances, after which they partook of some refreshments in an adjoining room, and then left for London.

Royal Christmas Fare

25 December, 1843

At Her Majesty's dinner table, the chief dish, according to 'good old English custom', was a splendid baron of beef, nearly four feet long, and between two and three feet in width, and weighing 180 pounds. There was also placed upon one of the side tables a hump of a Brahmin ox, presented to Her Majesty by Viscount Combermere, weighing 28 pounds.

Charitable Economy in the Royal Household

22 February, 1844

At the suggestion of Her Majesty, a distribution, to be continued three times a week in future, was commenced to the several alms houses within the burgh of Windsor, of cut and unused pieces of bread from the Royal Household. It was arranged that the whole of the cut but unused pieces of bread, thoughout the various departments of the Royal residence, daily amounting to a very large quantity, should in future, instead of being wasted by being consigned to the washtub, to feed the pigs of those domestics who had the privilege of participating in a perquisite of this nature, be given to the inmates of the several alms houses within the burgh, about thirty in number.

Departure of the Emperor of Russia

10 June, 1844

The presents distributed by the Emperor of Russia during his stay in England were most numerous, and of great value. Every individual who had ministered in any way, however humble, to the service or comfort of the Emperor, was rewarded according to his deserts. To each of the principal heads of the Queen's Household (sixteen in number) the Emperor presented a magnificent gold snuff-box, with a beautifully executed enamel portrait of His Majesty, surrounded by diamonds. The equerries and grooms-in-waiting upon the Emperor were presented with boxes of a similar description, surmounted by the Imperial cypher, set in brilliants.

To the three chief officers of the Royal Mews, the Emperor presented massive gold boxes. A variety of smaller gold boxes, watches, and rings were left by His Majesty at the disposal of the master of the Household, the Hon. Mr Murray, for presentation to the principal domestics under his direction; while the munificent sum of £2,000 was given by the Emperor to be divided among the servants employed in the departments severally presided over by the Lord Steward, the Lord Chamberlain, and the Master of the Horse. The Emperor gave 1,000 guineas to the Society for the Relief of Foreigners in Distress; £500 to the Nelson Testimonial Fund; £500 to the Wellington Testimonial Fund; a piece of plate, to the value of £500, to be annually run for at Ascot Races; 200 guineas to the poor of St George's parish; 100 guineas towards the formation of an Hospital for Distressed Germans in London. The Emperor also left a munificent sum for distribution among the domestics at the Russian Embassy. The Commissioners of Police, the various officials in the office of the Consul-general, the captain of the barge which put the Emperor ashore, the labourers who put the carriages and baggage on board the steamer, and others were similarly remembered.

Early Rising—Force of Royal Example

16 September, 1844

In pursuance of the example of Her Majesty—whose piper, we are told, is employed to sound the pibroch every morning at 7 o'clock under the windows of Blair Castle—a few of the inhabitants of Newington have engaged a piper to perform a similar service to that neighbourhood. The piper commenced his duty on Tuesday, and is to continue to serenade the inhabitants until further notice every morning between 7 and 8 o'clock. Arrangements, we hear, are also in progress to effect the same object in George's Square; and we hope that other parts of the town will speedily follow this salutary example.

Deer Slaughtering

25 September, 1844

Undeterred by previous disappointment, the Royal party in the afternoon paid another visit to Glen Tilt, and this time with more assurance of success than before, so far as the shooting of deer was concerned. It appeared that, on the previous night, the deerhounds had been let slip on two deer; and after a chase of many hours, continued all night, over precipices and through ravines, had succeeded at last in bringing them to bay in the channel of the Tilt, where, surrounded by deerhounds, shepherds' dogs, and curs of every degree, that filled the glen with their hideous cries, the poor animals were quite hemmed in. Word was then sent down to Prince Albert at the Castle that the deer were at his mercy; and accordingly, after luncheon, the Prince and other members of the suite proceeded up the glen to witness the death of the deer. The poor creatures were soon slaughtered by His Royal Highness, their carcases being deposited on the backs of horses and borne in triumph to the Castle.

Lending the Queen an Umbrella

19 October, 1844

As the Queen and Prince Albert were taking a walk at Cowes, they were caught in a heavy shower of rain at a shelterless part of the hill commanding a view of the east. An aged postman, observing their predicament, and quite unaware of their rank, ran after them and tendered the use of his old gingham umbrella, which was graciously accepted, and the postman was invited to follow their footsteps to Osborne House. On his arrival at the portico, the postman was made aware that it was to his Royal Mistress he had thus the honour of offering this seasonable shelter, by having tendered to him Her Majesty's thanks and a £5 note, together with his old umbrella.

Accident to the Crown

9 August, 1845

The Queen drove in State from Buckingham Palace to the Houses of Parliament to close the session in person. Immediately after Her Majesty had delivered her speech, and was about to quit the House of Lords, the Duke of Argyle, whose office was to bear the velvet cushion on which the Crown was placed when the Queen was retiring, stumbled, causing the Crown to fall off the cushion to the floor. A number of the jewels fell out of it, and it was otherwise injured. The jewels were all picked up and handed to the noble Duke.

—From the columns of *The Morning Post*, *The Morning Chronicle*, *The Morning Herald*, *The Scotsman*, etc. etc.

5 The Boy Beneath the Sofa

In the romantic glow of the early Victorian era, no one gained popular celebrity more readily than the record Palace intruder, the Boy Jones, In-I-Go Jones, the boy beneath the Queen's sofa.

The early Victorians dearly loved a Christmas story. The year of the young Queen's accession also saw the volume publication of *The Pickwick Papers*, and surely no gift was more welcome that Christmas than the book that contained the immortal festivities at Dingley Dell. Six years later, when the Queen and her guests sat down to "a splendid baron of beef, nearly four feet long", the Christmas of 1843 also marked the resounding triumph of *The Christmas Carol*. And set between these highlights of the Christmas spirit, between the inimitable Mr Jingle and cheerful Bob Cratchit, newspaper readers were constantly regaled with the seasonable real-life exploits of the Boy Jones, the urchin who intruded again and again into Buckingham Palace, the uninvited Christmas guest who sat upon the throne.

His escapades created a sensation—with an intriguing undercurrent of plot and counter-plot—and won him undying fame. Every Victorian family read of his adventures with an enjoyment punctuated by incredulous exclamations—the Boy Jones again! The young Queen Victoria was the first monarch to occupy the new Buckingham Palace, endowing it immediately with a youthful and romantic aura, and into that gilded and rose-carpeted world the Boy Jones trespassed with all the persistence of a moth to the flame.

"I roam about Windsor, raving with love for the Queen," Charles Dickens had written in fun, but the Boy seemed to express the popular fervour in close-up reality. And if a cat could look at the Queen, it caught the Victorian fancy to see that an urchin might do so as well, peeking and peering about the royal homestead without too much difficulty.

The Boy Jones lived within half a mile of the Palace, in the teeming parish of St James's. Behind the lively shops of Jermyn Street, up a staircase at 16 Bell Yard, his tailor father sat hunched over his sewing from dawn till dusk and his mother ironed and pressed to help support her brood of children. The streets of London, indeed, were his playground; and all the pageantry of Queen Victoria's early reign, the royal comings and goings, the carriage processions, the mounted Guards, were no more than his accustomed entertainment, the privileged street shows of a Cockney child.

When the Jones boy said, as he often did, that one day he would go to Buckingham Palace to see the grand staircase, his parents smiled. Such an ambition for such a young innocent! As a lad of twelve, puny and undersized, he could have squeezed unnoticed between the soldiers lining the fresh-gravelled streets to see the Queen riding in her gold state coach to her Coronation. Promoted and out and about in the world as an errand boy of thirteen, he may have cheered and shivered among the crowds on the freezing November morning when the Queen, having announced her betrothal to Prince Albert, rode out with the Prince to review her troops in Hyde Park. Among all her loyal subjects, the Queen could not have aroused a more intense interest than her effect upon the Boy Jones. But on 12 December, 1839, the Boy Jones undoubtedly went too far, and when he failed to return home that night from his employer's shop in Coventry Street his worried mother never dreamed that he was indeed in the Palace and snugly asleep—though coated in soot—in the fresh-made bed of the absent Master of the Household.

How the Boy Jones entered Buckingham Palace remains an unsolved mystery to this day. Security was lax, and perhaps some crony had hinted that it would be easy enough for "a young 'un and a little 'un" to pass unnoticed in the traffic of scullions and grooms and even chimney-sweeps at the kitchen entrance. Possibly some boon companion, an apprentice, a bootboy or an older member of the kitchen staff, entertained him among the pots and pans with a nod and wink to others. The one certainty is that eventually the Boy Jones found himself incredibly alone in a stone-flagged corridor, stealing breathlessly past open doors, skipping into hiding whenever he caught a distant glimpse of a liveried servant, and exploring the Palace for all he was worth.

All unaware of its existence, he skirted the Aladdin's cave of the gold-and-silver pantry and came to the suite of ground-floor bedrooms reserved for equerries and higher officials. As it happened, the Court was at Windsor and none of the rooms he entered on tiptoe were occupied. His senses tingling, young Edward Jones must have gasped at the softness of turkey rugs, at the sheen of mahogany in the moonlight, the lush comfort of cushioned armchairs. When a growing radiance of candlelight warned him that someone was coming, he tried to hide in a fireplace, as he confessed, and wildly scrambled from the hot grate into the chimney itself.

When he emerged, scattering soot in every direction, all was quiet. It was also much darker and, in the apartments of Sir Charles Murray, Master of the Household, the Boy could judge the luxury of the silken curtains only by fingering them, relish the armchairs only by sitting in them and enjoy Sir Charles's scented pomadeonly by spreading it on his own sooty hair. He could savour the softness of the bed only by trying it and, sinking into the unimaginable luxury of goosedown and linen, *he fell asleep*.

The next morning, just before five o'clock, Mr Will Cox, the porter, was dozing in a chair in his room at the Equerries' Entrance when, as he said, a boy "having the appearance of a sweep" half-opened his door. "And which chimney have you come to sweep, my lad?" asked Mr Cox. Whereupon the boy bolted, with police, porters and footmen soon in hot pursuit, following the trail of soot marks that led irresistibly to Sir Charles Murray's bedroom. There the bed was "found to be in confusion, the sheets covered with soot, the curtains sooty, likewise the furniture." And there was the incriminating evidence, as Mr Cox testified, that "on a floor nearby was a sword, a seal and a couple of books, made up into a bundle as if for speedy removal".

And so the Boy Jones made his public debut, peering like Oliver Twist over the dock of a magistrate's court and charged with "being found in the Palace and with stealing a sword and other articles, the property of Her Majesty." He had armoured himself with a false name, pretending to be Edward Cotton, up from the country, from the self-same district, indeed, from which Oliver Twist had commenced his runaway journey to London. "I came from Hertfordshire," he said, on being ordered to give an account of himself, "and was let into the Palace by a man dressed in fustian (plain clothes)."

"Why did this man let you in?" enquired Mr White, the magistrate.

"Oh, I can't account for that."

An intelligent boy, tolerably well educated, the magistrate, noted, but also a boy of vivid imagination, perhaps not to be believed. He took note that "the accused claimed he had been in the Palace before." . . . "And a very comfortable place I found it. I used to hide behind the furniture and up the chimneys in daytime. At night I walked about, went to the kitchen and got my food. I have seen the Queen and her Ministers in Council, and have heard all they said."

"Do you mean to say," Mr White interposed, "you have worn but one shirt all the time?"

"Yes, when it was dirty, I washed it out at night in the kitchen."

The court shook with laughter.

"The apartment I like best is the drawing-room — —"

Louder laughter still. The prisoner, indeed, "seemed to regard the whole proceeding as good fun". Mr White enquired severely whether he had any relations. "I lived in the city of Hertford with Mr H. Cotton, shoemaker and a householder there."

Mr White: Is he any relation?

"Only my father."

Again the laughter, and Mr White said sternly, "You are not a sweep, are you?"

"Oh, no. My face and hands are dirty from sleeping in chimneys. No, I don't know the names of any servants. But I know my way all over the Palace and have been in the Queen's apartments and all. The Queen"—and this the Boy added as a parting proof of his intimate knowledge—"the Queen is very fond of politics!"

(CASA DE PORTUGAL)

Prince Ferdinand's architectural extravaganza: the Pena Palace, Sintra.
(See THE OTHER PRINCE CONSORT)

The Boy upon the palace bed.
An exploration of royal corridors.

(See THE BOY BENEATH THE SOFA)

Reconstructions from the film *The Mudlark* (Twentieth Century-Fox)

Mr White considered the story "teeming with improbabilities" and directed that the police should make further enquiries. The boy was remanded, and the newspapers of course had a field day. From Bell Yard Henry Jones hurried in agitation to the police station to identify the prisoner as his son, Edward. From Coventry Street rushed Mr Thomas Griffiths, the grocer, to speak for his missing errand-boy. And in the Bell Tavern, next door to No. 16 Bell Yard, Mr James, the landlord, may well have trembled with guilty apprehension, for reasons we may examine later.

Edward Jones, aged fourteen, was committed for trial at the Westminster Assizes, where he appeared in January before a sensible English jury who laughed the case out of court. If Prosecuting Counsel decided behind the scenes that the property of the Queen could not have been stolen when the articles clearly belonged to Sir Charles Murray; if, too, it could be argued that nothing had been stolen merely by being wrapped in a bundle without being removed from the premises, there remained no case to answer but one of "mere folly". Besides, the proceedings were harshly unsuitable on the eve of the Queen's marriage. The Boy was acquitted, and nothing more might ever have been heard of him—except for the yearning that seized him at the approach of the following Christmas . . . and the altogether remarkable fact that *he did it again.*

Once more the young Queen happened to be much in the thoughts of her people, for her first child, the Princess Royal, had been born only two weeks earlier, and the public interest in the Royal Family now kindled the torch of sensation that blazed around Jones. Sir Charles Murray had been protesting for months that the garden wall of the Palace was "so low that any mischievous boy can scramble over it with the greatest ease", and so it proved. On Wednesday 2nd December one of the two larder cooks noticed finger-marks in the jelly of a cold jar of stock kept for soup. He told one of the eight master cooks who reported to the Royal Chef, who instituted a scathing enquiry among the twelve kitchen-maids and apprentices. And at first no one thought of the Boy.

On his own story to the police, which this time appeared to be true in almost every detail, he had first climbed the wall and crossed the unguarded lawns on the Monday night and entered the Palace by a French window but, as he said, "there were so many people moving about that I thought I had better go home." The next evening he had tried again, taking the same route over the lawns and through the same window, though not without leaving telltale mud stains at the threshold and not without cracking a glass pane when the French window suddenly swung behind him in the wind. No one noticed the clatter. That night the Boy Jones feasted unobserved in the kitchens, concealing himself behind bins and inside cupboards when he heard the watchman making his rounds. If the cooks had followed up the clue of the finger-marked stock next day, they would have found the Boy hidden under one of their beds in their own rooms just down the corridor.

He still had not seen the grand staircase but, not far from Sir Charles Murray's room, on his first visit, he had noticed and remembered a narrow stone stairway winding upwards. The haunting thought of that missed opportunity had dogged him ever since, and now he meant to explore the upper regions, come what may.

All that Wednesday was spent in hiding. Footmen stalked by unsuspecting as he crouched beneath tables or flattened himself in shadowy nooks and recesses. When night fell and all was silent, he found the service stairs just as he remembered and softly mounted the steps. Beyond an uninviting mezzanine floor, his way was barred by a door padded and bound in leather like a book and, cautiously pushing this open, he stepped into the breathtaking extravaganza of the state apartments.

How his heart must have thumped! It was the Palace as few have seen it, silent and deserted, patterned in shadow and silver beneath the skylights and latticed by moonlight except where a candle or two burned as nightlights in their sumptuous candelabra, glowing in gold. The Boy must have inhaled the smell of beeswax, paintwork and carpeting, as if it were heavenly incense. His boots felt swaddled and drugged in the incredible softness underfoot. He must have stood for minutes, just staring, his eyes questing over white and gold, over the sheen of polish and inlay, over crystal and porcelain.

He was, in fact, in the East Gallery. Close at hand a pair of glass doors opened on to the grand staircase as on to the slopes of a crimson-carpeted hillside, but lamplight and distant voices far below warned him of danger. His only route, then, was by way of the Silk Tapestry Room to the Picture Gallery. The unexpected sound of an ornamental clock, chiming midnight and sweetly and distantly echoed by other clocks, must have made him jump. Had he been only a few minutes earlier, he would have perhaps encountered the gaunt form of Lehzen, the Queen's governess, making her round to ensure that no danger threatened her treasure. As things were, there was merely the first glimpse of white statuary to freeze him to the spot, ghostly and terrifying, until his quivering senses could reassure him.

Under the gaze of the portraits and the glimmering sheen of the pictures the Boy moved down the Gallery until he realised that something else, another shadow, moved ahead of him, slipping like himself from one velvet blackness to another. Watching and waiting, he discovered he was ambushing nothing more than his reflection in the mirrored doors at the far end. But the disquieting image caused him to turn right . . . into a gold-and-crimson apartment, where the crystals of six huge chandeliers reflected the window-light and he realised that he stood in the Throne Room.

The Boy Jones could not resist climbing the dais and sinking into the crimson cushions. It seems that he may have sat upon the throne, dreaming his dreams, for almost an hour. Then he could not resist trying to see what lay beyond and so, feeling his way along the damask walls, he stepped through the pass-door leading into the private apartments. A long passage confronted him, and presently he heard an unexpected but familiar sound, the wail of a crying baby.

The Queen's nurse, Mrs Lilly, was lightly asleep in an ante-room to the Queen's dressing-room when she heard a door creak. Raising her head, she called "Who's there?" but no one answered and the door continued stealthily opening. Mrs Lilly called again and the door was suddenly shut from the other side. Certain that something was wrong, the nurse tugged the bell-rope for the page and then, with some presence of mind, bolted the door on her own side. Lehzen and the Queen's page, Kinnaird, were promptly on the scene and entered the dressing-room together. As Lady Longford, the Queen's biographer, has said, "Kinnaird, no hero, looked under the Queen's sofa and hurriedly backed away. The valiant Lehzen, however, pushed the sofa aside and revealed a boy."

The Queen could scarcely have slept through the commotion. "Supposing he had come into the bedroom—how frightened I should have been," she confided to her journal next day.

But Jones was harmless. The police searched him and were mystified to find that he carried no dangerous weapon, not even a pen-knife. Was he then bent upon robbery? No royal property was found on him, either. The Boy was not repeating his previous mistake of attempting to carry off souvenirs in a bundle, not he. Now that the inevitable discovery had befallen him, in fact, the Boy Jones faced his captors with extraordinary composure. "Be polite to me," he admonished them, blandly. He had entered the Palace, he explained, simply because he wished to write about it, and he guilelessly showed Police-Inspector Stead how he had made his way from south to north across its length. He had "heard the Princess Royal squall" and sat upon the throne, he said, and there was the cracked window and the crumpled royal cushions to help confirm every word.

Before daybreak, however, with second thoughts, he began embroidering his story. Now he claimed to have entered the Palace by climbing to the roof and descending a chimney, though his clothes on this occasion bore no trace of soot. From beneath the sofa, he declared, he had heard the Queen and Prince Albert in conversation. The only truth to be gleaned from this was that the Queen had sat upon that very sofa three hours previously, "a sofa of the most costly material and workmanship," as the *Times* explained.

The authorities decided to avoid the publicity of a police-court hearing by holding a private inquiry before the Privy Council but, of course, the news was out. To invade the Palace *once* was an incident, to do so *twice* made the incident international, and a new shout of laughter went up. "The subject engrosses public attention. Nothing else is talked of," commented the *Times*. In the minor local excitement of his son's first Palace entry, Mr Jones, Senior, had found his tailoring skill so much in demand that he had opened a workship in Derby Street, Westminster, to cope with the eager flow of inquisitive customers. Now his workshop was besieged with reporters, policemen, would-be clients and jostling crowds. "I am requested by a high authority not to answer questions," Mr Jones told all and sundry. Which merely added fuel to the fire.

The whole country was astonished and dismayed by the proved lack of security around the Queen. Plasterers, plumbers and carpenters were still rambling her newly-completed Palace, and the police might know at sight those employed by the Lord Chamberlain but could not "personally know" all those employed by the Board of Works. The *Annual Register* recorded soberly that the proximity of the Boy had not disturbed the Queen and "a few hours of rest tended to the restoration of Her Majesty." (Indeed, she conceived the future King Edward VII a few weeks later.)

For a week the Boy Jones languished in the House of Correction in Westminster, deriving comfort, it is to be hoped, by being able to see through the bars the familiar shop of his current employer, a chemist in Tothill Street. There was scant other consolation. His father bitterly complained in print that the boy was denied "either access to his friends or the assistance of counsel and . . . tried by a secret court . . . a novel and un-English mode." Mr Henry Jones would have been even more deeply indignant had he known that his son had been given a sample of the treadmill . . .

"And how do you like the punishment?" one of the Boy's interrogators demanded. The lad replied philosophically that he "had got into the scrape and must do the best he could."

The press were in fact excluded from the Privy Council hearing at the Home Office on 13 December. Mr Pickwick was never regarded with greater sternness by Justice Stareleigh and Sergeant Busfuz than the Boy Jones as he faced an overpowering tribunal consisting of the Marquis of Normanby, the Home Secretary; the Earl of

Erroll, the Lord Steward; the Earl of Uxbridge, the Lord Chamberlain; Lord Duncannon; Mr Fox-Maule, M.P., Under-Secretary of State; Mr Hall, the Chief Magistrate of Bow Street; and Colonel Rowan, the Commissioner of Police. Clearly, this was not a formally appointed Council, but neither was it a trial for, as Mr Jones, Snr. later protested, "hearing only one side of the question cannot be called so".

Probably only Mr Hall, the magistrate, possessed powers of summary justice, doubtful as it is whether these were properly exercised on this occasion behind closed doors. No one gave evidence on the Boy's behalf, even his father being excluded from this unusual court. Mr Jones could otherwise have testified, as he did later to the press, that his son had "never committed a dishonest act" although he possessed "a remarkable curiosity". Diminutive between two policemen, the Boy could only plead that it was simple to enter the Palace if one wanted to write a book . . . and Mr Hall fiercely sentenced him to three months imprisonment as "a rogue and a vagabond".

And so the Boy Jones returned to the House of Correction, that new-built model establishment for setting rogues and vagabonds to work, where 300 boys were housed in a model way two to a cell, models indeed for the thirty desperate incorrigibles—aged ten to fifteen—who were kept in the stygian horror of the "dark cells" below ground. The model statistics disclosed that only 150 boys of the 300 were unavoidably on the sick list; and the Boy Jones, in his father's words, entered the model prison "stout and strong, and came out thin as a skeleton, sinking under the effects of over-work and under-diet".

The Boy, indeed was enabled to slim on the treadmill, treading the 7½-inch revolving steps for six hours a day, three hours at a time, steadying himself by a hand-rail, on the treads for fifteen minutes and resting for five, inescapably treading and toiling until he had climbed the daily statutory 8,640 feet, less than half the height of Mont Blanc but higher each day than if he had climbed Snowdon and Ben Nevis combined.

Three and a half thousand paces a day, nothing to an experienced errand boy, but wearying as one grew weaker and more fatigued, hour by hour, isolated within creaking wooden walls and deafened by the uproar and clatter, the oaths and commands, as the imprisoned boys desperately shouted to one another across their partitions. Treading and stumbling, his grand staircase substituted with satanic irony, the plodding Boy Jones must have slipped into his day-dreams of Buckingham Palace and of the soft, gilded and level expanses of the ground floor, which he had still not explored. Did he resolve to show them that they had not broken his spirit, not broken, indeed, his young heart? The grinding din of the treadmill, the floor ever wheeling and slipping beneath one's feet. . . . How indeed do you like your punishment, Boy, as the limbo of Christmas slips away into February and March?

Shortly before the Boy's release, Mr Hall, the magistrate, interviewed him and asked if he would like to go "on board a ship", and, to his utter astonishment, Jones coolly began to stipulate conditions.

"But would you not like to be sent to sea?" the magistrate persisted.

"It will be time enough to talk of that," the Boy Jones stoutly maintained, "when I am sent home."

Whereupon Mr Hall summoned young Edward Jones' parents to Bow Street and coaxed them into agreeing that their son might go to sea, persuasively signing an Order for them to visit the prisoner for the first time in the House of Correction, 'since they were sensible'. But this proved to be a psychological blunder. When Mrs Jones set eyes on her gaunt and wretched boy she burst into tears, pleading frantically that he was still a mere child and that it would be unduly harsh to send him from home. Besides, she now learned, her son had by no means given his own consent. This flung a very different light on the matter, and Justice Stareleigh could not have frowned more irritably on Mr Pickwick than Mr Hall when, as Mr Jones wrote mildly, "he upbraided us for changing our minds, and told us we might go away".

A day or two later, all the world read of the Boy Jones' liberation, "his term of imprisonment having expired". Crowds jostled and pushed in Bell Yard, hoping to catch a glimpse of him. A theatre impresario offered the immense sum of eighty shillings a week, plus the proceeds of a benefit performance, if only the Boy would make his bow to the audience during a specially written play to be entitled *Intrusion—or the Unwanted Guest*. Reporters jingled their sovereigns persuasively. It was before the days of the 'exclusive story', but the Boy would not say a word.

Meanwhile, the landlord of the Bell, Mr James, mopped his brow while serving the huge influx of thirsty, inquisitive customers and, again, alternately shivered with apprehension lest the Boy—and his troublesome tenants—should tell all they knew.

A clue for the reporters may well have lurked in the palatial candle-ends with which Mr James illuminated his tavern, or the fine quality biscuits his patrons munched, or his liberal helpings of pie. The *Times* was near the mark when it hinted that the Boy might not have broken into the Palace at all but might be "acquainted with some of the scullery boys or others of the kitchen". The truth, it seems, was that Mr James had a relative on the Palace staff entitled to candle-ends and small returned edibles from the royal table. But the perquisites of royal servants by no means extended to hundreds of candles a week or uncarved hams or tasty, entire pork-pies. If Mr James trafficked profitably in Palace victuals, it seems certain that he equally threatened his tailor tenant, the hapless Mr Jones, with instant eviction if any of his family breathed a word.

It redounds to the Boy Jones's credit that he disliked to talk of his Palace exploits. A rich American breezily offered to help such a "sharp, enterprising lad" to make his fortune overseas but, on calling at Bell Yard, was disappointed to meet "a small and sickly urchin, remarkable only for his taciturnity". The Boy sadly began to experience the penalties of fame. "No one will employ me," he told his father, "as soon as they see I was the boy that was in the Palace". With no little insight, the tailor wrote to a Sunday newspaper, expressing the fear that the Palace furore preyed on his son's mind. And presently the Boy Jones, indeed, could no longer resist the over-powering compulsion to do *the one thing he knew he should not do* . . .

His third trespass occurred on the night of 15 March, 1841, and the printing presses again hammered out his name—"Another Intrusion" . . . "Third Appearance of the Boy Jones at Buckingham Palace"—while London rang with witticisms about "In-I-Go Jones, the brilliant surveyor". Once again, so the Boy asserted, he had merely climbed over the wall and his route, to be sure, appeared to stem from the same south-west corner, by way of the equerries' rooms and kitchen quarters into the milky-marble, crimson-carpeted wonderland of the Grand Hall. In the months since his second visit, however, security had been increased by the strength of two police-sergeants of A Division who took turn to patrol the building at night. This additional precaution proved the Boy's undoing.

Shortly after the Palace clocks had chimed 1 a.m., the duty sergeant saw a face peeping at him through the glass doors and, the next moment, the Boy ran full-tilt against him like a startled hare. He had taken off his boots, and in a nook behind the sculptures scraps of cold meat and potatoes were found spread upon a white handkerchief, a picnic which the journalists joyously described as "feasting on Her Majesty's larder".

Yet the reporters gleaned the details only from Palace gossip. Under the high-sounding pretext that an inquiry connected with royalty could not be held in a police-court, the Boy was tried in camera at the Home Office, with much the same Privy Council members as before to form a quorum. According to the *Times*, the Boy affected the greatest indifference. No witness was called except his captor, and the harassed parents had to wait in the street to hear that their son had again been sentenced to three months in the House of Correction.

But this time Mr Jones, senior, was not so readily silenced, having discovered that he had only to pick up his pen to enlist the sympathy of the papers. Was it right, he enquired, that the boy should be punished in prison for his stupid curiosity, while those responsible for protecting the Queen's palace should be retained there? Was it indeed proper for his son to be convicted without assistance for his defence?

Public opinion, hitherto amused at the Boy, felt that indeed it was not, and the fun became tempered with a sense of injustice. In June, when he had climbed his 700,000 stairs and was released from the House of Correction, his behaviour having been "quiet, orderly and even exemplary", the newspapers were vigilant. A whisper that the Boy was to be put aboard the *Diamond*, an emigrant ship sailing from the Thames to Australia, caused the *Times* to enquire acidly into "this very strange affair . . . this deportation" and, not surprisingly, no one talked to the newspapermen more guardedly than the landlord of the Bell. Murmuring pleasantly that he knew a friend, a ship's agent, who could help to put the Boy upon a very good ship, Mr James was careful to conceal from all the Jones family that the friend was in reality Inspector J. C. Evans of the Thames police, acting under explicit Home Office instructions.

Meanwhile, the King and Queen of the Belgians were paying a visit to the Queen, and no one watched the carriage processions on Constitution Hill with closer interest than the Boy himself, while no one watched the Boy Jones more keenly than the police. At the Home Office, the Marquis of Normanby sighed with deep relief when he heard that the miscreant, in the care of his good friends, Evans and James, had at last left London for Gravesend.

Unluckily, they missed the boat. The emigrant ship *Diamond* had already sailed with its cargo of hopeful human souls, but the agents hinted that she might call at Plymouth and James and Evans, with their young charge, hurried in pursuit. Plymouth was reached, but the *Diamond* had not put in, although there was certain news that she would now call at Cork. Nothing for it, then, but to sail in pursuit on a small Irish freighter only to learn, after sighting the crowded masts and church-spires of Cork, that they had irretrievably missed the *Diamond* again.

Mr James must have groaned aloud. No innkeeper had ever surely travelled so far to conceal defects in his catering. Then, at the eleventh hour, no doubt in some waterside tavern, he chanced to meet a Captain Ramsay, skipper of the *Tiber*, a sailing ship due to take on cargo before a five-months voyage to Brazil, and suddenly his troubles appeared at an end.

For a consideration, Captain Ramsay did not scruple to apprentice a boy to the sea for five years and ask no questions. No one will probably ever know how the Boy was abducted or under what threats or persuasions he signed his indentures. Of his voyage across the South Atlantic we can discover only that he told his father he was "subject to much ill-usage and quite disgusted with the seafaring life". At the end of November, when the *Tiber* returned to Liverpool from Bahia, Captain Ramsay may have imagined that his apprentice would not get far with empty pockets. But the Boy Jones knew how to pick up pennies by running errands at the new railway station, and as soon as he had funds of half-a-crown he blithely set out to walk to London.

When no better bed could be found, the lad slept in barns and outhouses. When his funds were exhausted, he staved off hunger by gnawing turnips from the half-frozen fields. He covered the 210 miles in eighteen days and, happy but exhausted, reached home in time for Christmas. At this point, the newspapers obviously considered that the topic of the Boy Jones had reached a happy ending. "He never alludes to his visits to the Palace," one disappointed writer noted, "and is reluctant to converse with anyone on the subject". Early in the New Year, according to the *Times*, Jones was "placed in a comfortable situation", making himself useful about the coffee-rooms and cigar shop kept by a Mr Elgar nearly opposite Westminster Abbey, where he was "treated with the greatest kindness by his master and the customers". And then, in February, 1842, national excitement blazed around him once more and the headlines blared the announcement, "Extraordinary Disappearance of the Boy Jones!"

All the circumstances were indeed extraordinary. After coming home unexpectedly from the coffee-rooms in mid-morning, the Boy had asked his mother for a clean shirt and had not returned. His father had hurried feverishly to the police, and a posse of constables, even more agitated, had rushed to Buckingham Palace but though they searched every hiding-place the boy was not to be found. The news-hungry—and thirsty—reporters once again crowded the Bell. It is difficult not to paint the landlord as the villain of the piece, for Mr James watched the frantic anxiety of the parents and knew where the boy was—and yet said nothing. Still desperately concerned with his own safety, the unscrupulous James had, in fact, successfully spirited young Jones away.

Several days elapsed before the worried tailor received a mysterious and anonymous letter. Signed merely, "a Captain, and Well-Wisher to Your Son" it was brief, if reassuring. "Sir—I am requested by your son Edward to inform you he sailed on board the —— for America on Friday last, and he wishes you to remember him to his old and faithful friend, Mr James . . ."

Reassuring . . . and yet a disquieting missive, too, with its indication that the Boy was prevented from writing, the name of the ship left blank, and its inner hint implicating Mr James. However, the Boy's ingenuity was fully equal to circumventing any censorship. That same day the kindly Mr Elgar received a letter in the boy's own handwriting, postmarked from Portsmouth, and telling of a conversation with Mr James, who had a friend to offer him "a good situation" at sea. "I declared that I was provided with a good Sittiation," wrote the Boy, "and sickened with the sea". There had nevertheless been a meeting at Vauxhall Bridge, full of implicit threat and persuasion. "The same day we was at Portsmouth. The following morning I was before the Captain Lord John Hay of the 52-gun frigate *Warspite* . . . and he told Mr James' friend to purchase a Suit of Blue. Now I am on board, aware that I am bound to serve four years or more as a seaman. The ship is bound to North America, a cold climate . . ."

Before Mr Elgar could read these words, the *Warspite* had sailed. The circumstances of the Boy Jones' entry into the Royal Navy seemed, as the newspapers said, to have been highly dubious" but, like Mr Micawber, Mr Jones, Snr. was "in such reduced circumstances as to be unable to take just measures." Once again Mr James could breathe freely and continue his traffic in Palace comestibles, though not for as long as he had anticipated. Seven months later, he heard one morning that someone wished to see him and there stood, not the Boy Jones, but a sturdy Seaman Jones, now a strong and masculine young man of eighteen with something of special force and directness to say to him.

The *Warspite* having returned to Portsmouth, Jones lost little time in raising funds by selling his "coat of blue" for 45s. and walking to London. And having seen his old friend and worst enemy, Mr James, he appeared indifferent when the police arrived at his parents' home to conduct him back to his ship.

The Boy Jones had at last sailed through the pangs of adolescence. The *Warspite* presently set sail for the Mediterranean and we hear of Seaman Jones serving as mizzen-topmast-man. No one on board could swarm up the rigging with greater sureness: he owed it to the treadmill that he became a good climber. From the mast heights he experienced the authentic thrill of adventure when he watched the bombardment of Tunis by French men-o'-war, an action in which the British warships "stood by". His officers reported his conduct as "orderly and regular".

Probably the only exception was a night when the frigate decks heard the cry of "Man overboard". Jones had either dived or fallen. Rescued while clinging to a lighted buoy, he explained that he had "leaned too far" while trying to see how it worked. "His mates," wrote Lord John Hay, "think that he did it on purpose. He is a singular character."

In May, 1846, when the *Warspite* was returning to Chatham, it was deemed best that Jones should remain at a safe distance, and at Malta he was transferred for further Mediterranean service aboard the *Inconstant*. There we may end this Dickensian tale. Grown bulky and good-looking, he could successfully pretend not to be the celebrated Boy Jones, Edward Jones: his friends, indeed, knew him as Edwin. He had long since slaked his thirst for Buckingham Palace . . . the busy kitchens, the moonlit Picture Gallery, the Marble Hall at midnight, the dreamlike and yet irrefutable occasion when he had sat alone upon the throne.

—The Times, The Standard, Globe, etc. etc.
Home Office and Admiralty archives at the Public Record Office, the library of the Ministry of Defence, etc.

THE PRESENT REIGN

6 The Debut of Prince Philip

Positively the first public appearance of the Queen's husband in England, complete with overtones of the auspicious events to come . . .

One day in the shining August of 1934 the residents of Cromer—the seaside resort some thirty miles east of Sandringham—unfolded their local newspapers to find an announcement blazoned across two advertising columns of the front page to the effect that "the Greatest Gymkhana ever held in Norfolk" was to be staged at the Norfolk Riding School. It was to be in aid of the 'Crab-Boat Disaster Fund' and florid heavy type emphasized the alluring fact that the "Presentation of Prizes would be by H.R.H. Prince Philip of Greece". Local people who prided themselves on being fairly well informed on royal events and even on the affairs of the Greek Royal Family were faintly puzzled. The bachelor King George of Greece frequently stayed in the vicinity and was indeed in the neighbourhood at the time. But who was Prince Philip?

Then, by a felicitous coincidence, the news broke on the very eve of the gymkhana that the highly popular Prince George, the Duke of Kent, King George V's youngest son, was to marry Princess Marina of Greece. The engagement was greeted with tremendous enthusiasm and in consequence the topicality attracted a huge crowd to Cabbell Park, eager to see this mysterious Prince Philip, who must at least be Marina's close cousin and might even prove, the more romantic hoped, to be her tall and handsome and perhaps hitherto unknown brother. Instead, H.R.H. Prince Philip of Greece turned out to be a grinning and bashful thirteen-year-old schoolboy in a crumpled sports jacket and baggy trousers who nevertheless proceeded to hand out prizes and rosettes with superb aplomb.

Looking back, we may find it strangely prophetic that Prince Philip's first public appearance on royal duty should have been an equestrian and a sporting occasion, linked with royal romance and with the Sandringham countryside, enhanced by unmistakable overtones of public service and even by the adventurous tang of the sea. Ostensibly, Commander Oliver Locker-Lampson—who lived at Cromer—had engineered the event as a Cheam old boy. Prince Philip had come through Cheam prep school and his intermediate year at Salem and now was about to begin his first term at Gordonstoun. But coming events surely cast their impalpable shadows that sunny evening as the Commander gravely thanked Prince Philip for distributing the prizes and called on the crowd to give him three rousing cheers.

This summer-holiday lark raised over £200 for the Crab-Boat Fund, a sum comparable with the local takings of Sir Alan Cobham's air circus, an event which had set the young Prince gasping a few days earlier. It was fun at Cromer that torrid August, swimming and riding, the spartan disciplines of Salem safely behind one and the prospective seamanship courses of Gordonstoun glowing with promise ahead.

Revised from 'H.R.H. Prince Philip,
Sportsman' *by Helen Cathcart.*

7 The Queen and the Horses

The first public visit of the Queen to a race-course—and the deeper motives of her racing enthusiasm.

The first public visit the Queen ever paid to a race-meeting was on Whit Monday, 21 May, 1945, when she was the nineteen-year-old Princess Elizabeth. It was a day of brilliant sunshine and the Ascot crowds were in rare holiday mood, buoyed by the supremely wonderful fact that the war in Europe had ended only a fortnight before. There were to be no more bombs, no more battles. There would soon be no more partings, no more austerity. The throng was jubilant, and a shock-wave of enthusiasm suddenly swept the stands when it was seen that two khaki-clad figures had quietly entered the Royal Box. There was a moment of initial doubt and then cheers broke out as King George VI and his daughter and Princess Marina, the Duchess of Kent, came forward to the rail and it was realised that they had come to share in the rejoicing and hard-won relaxation of the people.

The King was in his khaki Field-Marshal's uniform, the young Princess in uniform as an A.T.S. subaltern, dress of formal propriety in those days of mingled peace and war. The King had some doubt on attending the races, without the excuse of a classic event or one of his own runners, while hostilities still raged in the Far East. It was evident, from the preparation of the Royal Box a few minutes earlier, that it had been a last-minute decision. The Princess had no doubt been persuasive at the luncheon table. Racing began at noon, but there were still three or four events on the card and the royal party arrived just in time to see Gordon Richards win the Bray Stakes unchallenged on Neolight, that dashing filly who was so rarely to be beaten.

The delighted Princess Elizabeth was to be seen, asking insistent questions, pointing and gesticulating excitedly. She had previously visited the course and toured the administrative buildings when they were, so to speak, unoccupied and off-duty, concerned only with the preliminaries of a meeting. Now the spectacle burst into life and colour, with the shouting on the far side, the babble of comment, the pageantry of the jockeys and their mounts, the ever-changing flux of the crowds. Moving down to the paddock with her father, her pleasure was surely increased when she discovered that they were seldom recognized. Racegoers were intent on the tote and khaki was an inconspicuous dress among so many khaki-clad figures. The next race, the Finchampstead Handicap, provided a particularly good foretaste of all the sensations the Turf was to offer, for it was won by Historic—son of Solario—after being paced all the way, yard by yard over two miles, by an extremely consistent rival to win at last by a length. The colt had carried nine stone seven pounds over the extremely long course and, as soon as his heavy saddle was removed, he exuberantly rolled on the grass, to the Princess's great amusement.

Between the races, eager to see everything, she was privileged to enter the weighing-in room and she climbed energetically to the roof of the stand to share the view which staff from the royal palaces were enjoying with their own guest passes, gazing down at the greensward that ran like a river between the great banked patterns of people. Then came the Bisham Handicap, to be won by Sun Up, and finally the victory of the neatly named Kingstanding in the Binfield Stakes. Anxious to avoid an ovation, the King however insisted on leaving before the last race. The Princess was left with a sensation of precipitant excitement and went home to a late tea chatting eagerly of the day's events.

It became obvious that nothing could keep her away from the Derby to be held at Newmarket that June under wartime conditions. In the most enigmatic of races, the King's colt, Rising Light, was to be pitted against an intractable favourite, a certain Dante. In the light of events we know that Dante was to provide the north of England with its first Derby triumph in seventy years. The curtains of the future, however, remained inscrutably closed in that June sunshine and Rising Light had convincingly opened the season by easily winning the Column Stakes to the accompaniment, as a newspaper reported, of "much cheering and raising of hats". This had occurred on the day when the Americans crossed the Elbe, driving forward their spearhead to within seventy miles of Berlin, and the topical ring of Rising Light caught the interest now that the lights of Europe were flashing on.

Yet, above all, a more personal factor created the Princess's interest. In a very real sense she felt that Rising Light was almost her own horse, for she had patted him at the door of his foaling-box at Hampton Court and led him on one of his first walks through the arch of the great brick wall into the paddock. She had ingeniously helped to name him, by Hyperion out of Bread Card, and was convinced he was one of a group of newcomers from the Royal paddocks destined to affect the course of racing history.

At this point perhaps our narrative should change course itself and return to the mid-war period when the King was leasing the bulk of his horses from the National Stud and the fifteen-year-old Princess paid a visit to Beckhampton with her parents to watch the brightest hopes in training. Or perhaps one should glance back to the farther days of infancy when the Archbishop of Canterbury found the Princess leading King George V by the beard, pretending that he was a horse as he shuffled along the floor on hands and knees.

The Queen's love of horses can be readily traced to her earliest years. She was barely five when her governess, Marion Crawford, caught that first memorable glimpse of a small figure in the night nursery, the cords of her dressing-gown tied to the bedstead in lieu of reins, busily driving a team of imaginary horses around the park. Before long "Crawfie" herself was a horse, decked in a pair of red reins with jingling bells, playing earnest make-believe in response to childish entreaties, snuffling into a nosebag or pawing the ground.

Around the topmost landing of 145 Piccadilly stood some three dozen toy horses, the stabled accumulation of many a birthday and Christmas. Every evening each fondly named horse had to be fed and watered, its saddle comfortably removed. Every morning each was set in order. And there were rocking-horses to be eagerly mounted in the nursery at St Paul's Walden, toy horses and carts to be drawn along the grounds of Royal Lodge. This "obsession for toy horses," Miss Crawford reported of her pupil, "lasted unbroken until real horses became important". Then there were the horses still to be watched in the London streets at that time, huge draught horses drawing their brewer's drays towards Piccadilly, and tired ponies dragging costers' carts.

The sight of a pony with a docked tail would arouse royal indignation at the nursery windows. The hacks watched from another window, prancing along Rotten Row, became better known than their ever-changing riders. "If I am ever Queen," said Lilibet, strangely, "I shall make a law that there must be no riding on Sundays. Horses should have a rest."

Although his grand-daughter was only nine when he died, King George V contributed his own decisive influence. He was accustomed to go round the stables at Sandringham and Wolferton after lunch on Sundays, giving each yearling and mare a word and a pat. And his "sweet little Lilibet" sometimes accompanied him on these expeditions, to be gravely introduced to Scuttle (by Captain Cuttle) who had won the King his first and only classic race; to meet among the foals Felstone and Polonaise, Etiennette and Jubilee (who was subsequently to take the first royal victory of George VI's Coronation year) and to see Limelight, the impressive stallion, one-time winner of the Hardwicke Stakes.

Grown-ups would attempt to urge a moral and tell how, as a racehorse, Limelight liked to begin slowly and let his field lead him and then come at the end with a burst of speed to win his race. And there was the Sandringham statue of Persimmon as a reminder of events far beyond childhood's memory, eloquent to the little Princess that horses, too, were often great.

The old King gave the Princess her first pony, a Shetland named Peggy, when she was only four. She was lifted on to its back and by her fifth birthday was a sufficiently skilled rider to make at least a token appearance with the Pytchley. Her father wished to honour one of the hunt servants, Frank Freeman, who was retiring, by having his daughter "entered by the finest huntsman of his time", and for a few yards Peggy obligingly joined in the chase, so far as being led by a groom permitted. Henry Owen, the Duke of York's groom, found himself lavished with hero worship as the Princess grew a little older, accustomed to his riding lessons and well able to obey his constant injunctions to "Curl in underneath" or "Keep on your guard".

"Yes, of course, Owen," she would be heard saying. Indeed, Owen could do no wrong, and was for years quoted as a minor family oracle with "Owen says this..." or "Owen says that..." Until, at long last, when King George VI was being consulted on some future plan, he told his daughter, a trifle testily: "Don't ask me. Ask Owen. Who am I to make suggestions?"

When the family moved to Buckingham Palace, the toy horses were arrayed in the corridor outside the children's rooms, where they stood sentinel until after Princess Elizabeth was married. The Princesses also resumed their riding lessons and regular tutelage soon began with Mr Horace Smith, whose school at Holyport was one of the Windsor amenities. He found the elder sister already a fine rider, conscientious and thorough, and he came under a cross-fire of innumerable questions on stable management, feeding, and the methods of training horses. The Princess evidently found it advisable to check the knowledge she had already picked up in the Mews. As she grew in proficiency, the riding master tried her on a wide range of mounts, including many more difficult horses which she could scarcely have found a pleasure to ride. His pupil never questioned his choice or expressed her own preferences. "The Princess was painstaking," he pronounced. "An ideal pupil, she knew that it was all an essential part of her curriculum of instruction and she was more than anxious to learn." At thirteen, the Princess had already discovered her possible future position as Heiress Apparent: of importance some distant day, as she imagined, when Papa was old. To Smith she shyly confessed that if she were not who she was she would like to be "a lady living in the country with lots of horses and dogs".

Princess Elizabeth began to learn jumping on her pony Comet

and found that her Uncle Harry and Aunt Alice of Gloucester already had an unsuspected knowledge of technique. Aunt Mary, the Princess Royal, spasmodically appeared from Goldsborough with news of the Harewood racehorses. The Princess was entering more and more into adult conversation, discovering that amid the many fascinating new topics her own prime absorbing interest recurred. There was news of one of Papa's horses called Cosmopolitan who had very properly defeated another horse called King of the Air. On the day that Mr Chamberlain flew to Munich, Cosmopolitan ran in the Hopeful Stakes at Newmarket but was sadly reduced to second. So that, people said, the Stakes were not so hopeful after all. Many months later Cosmopolitan won the July Handicap and the Princess Royal, who watched the race, gave her niece a warm description of his gallant and rewarding effort.

The King and Queen went to Canada and the United States in 1939, missing both the Derby and Royal Ascot, so that the thirteen-year-old Princess heard little of these last pre-war events in racing. Crawfie made sure of a long spell of uninterrupted schoolroom routine. At Holyport Mr Smith noticed that the Princess appeared, rain or shine, for her riding lessons, but was whisked away the minute his lesson was due to end. Pursuing an exacting timetable, the studies with the Vice-Provost of Eton College had begun and the young Princess was deeply immersed in constitutional history.

On one occasion, however, when the Harewoods were staying at Egerton House, Newmarket, the Princess went to see her cousins and explored the stables and yards where her grandfather's and great-grandfather's horses had been trained. Persimmon, Diamond Jubilee, Minoru, Friar Marcus—the men still remembered the old names with affection.

Inside the archway leading to the main stable-yard the young Princess noticed at once the panel on which had been commemorated in letters of gold the races and stakes won by King Edward VII.

Year	Number of races won	Amount £
1893	2	372
1894	5	3,499

1895	11	8,281
1896	12	26,819

and so on for a tally of eighteen years, down to the impressive total of 106 races won for an amount of £134,687.

Was this the moment, amid the friendly stable smell of hay and soap and fodder, on familiar family ground, the moment above all others that first saw the stirring of Her Majesty's Turf ambitions? Did she recall that tablet under the dusky archway, one wonders, when she was grown to womanhood and owned one of the finest racing strings in the world?

In his best year, King Edward VII won only thirteen races, compared with the Queen's thirty victories—and £62,212 winnings—in 1957. All the gains commemorated in gilt at Egerton House were, in fact, outshone by the Queen's stake winnings of over £150,000 in her first ten years as owner. (She first registered her own racing colours in 1949 and first won the glorious sum of £81 in prize-money with a gift horse named Astrakhan, presented to her by the Aga Khan.)

It is often though that the Queen's racing luck has diminished; or, rather, that the successes of her second racing decade by no means compare with the first. The figures tell otherwise:

Year	Number of races won	Amount £
1959	16	38,154
1960	2	1,310
1961	11	13,029
1962	5	4.404
1963	11	13,467
1964	13	11,607
1965	19	43,627
1966	5	6,397
1967	14	13,522
1968	7	14,365
	Ten year total	£159,882

(*Revised from* 'The Queen and the Turf' *by Helen Cathcart.*)

8 Prince Philip's Mother

"My sister is an astonishing woman," said Earl Mountbatten. Yet, at her own insistence, Prince Philip's mother remains the least known member of the Royal Family.

From the inner tranquillity of her second-floor suite in Buckingham Palace, an old lady occasionally looks down at the distant flash of traffic in the Mall, glancing over the treetops to the spires and towers of one of the cities that she likes best in all the world. There are times when she sits in her fireside chair lost in a reverie of the past, for it is the privilege of an old lady to play tricks with the rolling years, and her nurses see her lips moving a little with the vigorous memory of a bygone conversation. And then Prince Charles or Princess Anne come to visit her, and her dark brown eyes glow with pleasure—for, nearing her eighty-sixth year, H.R.H. Princess Alice still takes an amused and lively interest in the events of today.

Prince Philip's mother—H.R.H. Princess Alice of Greece and Denmark—is at the very heart of the Royal Family. Every day, whenever she feels herself ready to receive visitors, her son is at her door, and his official schedule must be rigorous indeed for him to defer this morning call. With a comprehending and sympathetic eye, he knows at once whether his mother is tired or in lively mood. The Queen, too, enjoys slipping in with some pleasant item of family gossip, and Princess Alice invariably has news of her own to tell, drawn from the tide of correspondence with children and grand-children, nephews and nieces.

Her brother, Earl Mountbatten, is a regular visitor, ready to indulge her equally with present-day gossip or family reminiscences. He was the youngest son in the family in which she was the eldest daughter. Both are Mountbattens born—or Battenbergs, if you wish for precision—both gifted with the same energy and determination in vigorously following up every decision they make.

In clear contrast to the publicity that continually surrounds Earl Mountbatten, this explains why Prince Philip's mother remains curiously little-known to the public. It is a well-established precedent that the mother-in-law of the Sovereign should remain inconspicuous, but once Princess Alice had firmly decided in her own mind that her charitable work, pursued in a spirit of religious faith, mattered more than anything else, she completely withdrew from public affairs. Outside the family, few people were thus aware of the domestic landmark in her life when she unobtrusively took up residence in Buckingham Palace in the summer of 1967. She had been ill in a London hospital and was persuaded to prolong her holiday. "It was all a matter of sensibly deciding what would be for the best," a family friend has said. "We really knew she had settled in when she began surrounding herself with her family photographs from her old home in Athens."

Yet in sharing the private inner life of the Royal Family, Princess Alice has a deep and serene sense of belonging. In this very Palace, long ago, as a little girl, she shared the wedding excitement of the "Princess May" who became Queen Mary. Skipping with glee down the corridors, Princess Alice of Battenberg was one of the bridesmaids, looking "very sweet in white satin, with a little pink and red rose on the shoulder and some small bows of the same on the shoes," as Queen Victoria carefully noted at the time. A picture by Tuxen at the Palace shows little Alice intently watching the ceremony, and Buckingham Palace is indeed full of these tangible keepsakes of her yesterdays.

Not long ago her grandson, Prince Andrew, sent her a characteristically boyish letter from Heatherdown School to thank her for a birthday present, and his signature appeared to afford her a touchingly personal pleasure, for young Andrew was of course named after her husband, Prince Andrew of Greece. Often, at mid-week, her old friend, Lady Zia Wernher, will call in . . . and no one responds more sympathetically than Lady Zia to reminiscences of the old days, in Athens and Paris, in Stockholm and Russia, at Balmoral and Kensington Palace, and at Windsor Castle, where Princess Alice was born.

In her generation, Princess Alice was linked to the Royal Family—and indeed to nearly every other royal house of Europe—by a close meshwork of cousinhood, much as Princess Alexandra is today. Grandmama of our own Queen's children, as she is, her own grandmother was Queen Victoria's second daughter, an astonishing link in time. But perhaps we can find the beginning of the story in the youthful Queen Victoria's own words.

"Our little baby is to be called Alice, an old English name . . ." the Queen wrote to her Uncle Leopold in 1843. Plump little Alice, "Fat" and "Fatima", as she became known within the royal circle, Queen Victoria's second daughter nevertheless grew up a slim and comely pincess, and when she married Prince Louis of Hesse in 1862 their love-match in turn was blessed by the arrival of a daughter. Queen Victoria, middle-aged now and widowed, sat at the young mother's bedside, in the Lancaster Tower at Windsor Castle, and the baby whom she all but saw delivered was to become Princess Victoria of Battenberg, mother of Princess Alice and Earl Mountbatten.

And so the years rolled by and on a February day in 1885 we find Queen Victoria again waiting in the same room overlooking the Long Walk, and once more tending a young mother-to-be. At twenty-one, Princess Victoria had married the handsome Prince Louis of Battenberg, who was the first "Mountbatten" to join the Royal Navy and to become British by naturalisation. Sitting beside the young mother from seven o'clock that wintry morning until five in the afternoon, murmuring encouragement and stroking her arms, the Queen found all the circumstances of the birth "strange and affecting", for the baby, a Princess, was born in the same bed as the mother had been.

The Queen, we see, was presiding at the advent of a great-granddaughter, and the attendant Dr Duncan marvelled at her patience and powers of endurance. Yet Queen Victoria would undoubtedly have found her vigil still more rewarding if she could have known that, beyond the curtains of the future, a child of *this* new baby would be Prince Philip and that he would marry the next Queen Regnant, Queen Elizabeth II.

Travel has always marked the course of Princess Alice's life and, a true sailor's daughter, she first went aboard ship when only two months old, crossing the Channel in the royal yacht *Victoria and Albert* for her christening in Darmstadt. A concourse of royalty gathered at the family font of the Hesse and Battenberg line to hear her resoundingly named Victoria Alice Elizabeth Julie Marie and, for those intent on the signs and portents of these occasions, the auspices were bright. Even the Queen joined the family party, and the festivities were enhanced by the local celebrations for the betrothal of the Queen's youngest daughter, Princess Beatrice, to the baby's good-looking uncle, Prince Henry of Battenberg. The little town was gay with welcoming decorations, the Church bells pealed and fireworks blazed in the night sky.

The young parents settled that summer in a country house near Chichester named Sennicotts, and the stream of visitors included the beautiful Princess of Wales (later Queen Alexandra); the baby's Aunt Alix, who was to become the last Czarina of Russia, and her young cousin Sophie, who became Queen of Greece. Everyone admired the baby's fair hair and intent gaze and could agree with the fond mama that she was indeed "a fine sturdy child". Sennicotts was a haven of domestic bliss. "We are not blessed much with earthly goods, and have to live in a small way, though we are happier for it, I believe," Lord Louis wrote contentedly to a friend.

Then came a heart-rending discovery. Princess Victoria longed for the day when she could teach her little daughter to say "Papa" and "Mama" and the baby seemed slow in this primary accomplishment. She had always appeared indifferent to a tinkling musical-box but would pant with glee at what was probably a favourite plaything, a set of gay-coloured balls. The possibility that their child might not hear very well began to worry the Battenbergs and the doctors soon confirmed their worst fears. The infant Princess Alice was deaf and because she could have no idea of the world of sound there were fears that she might also be dumb.

It was a terrible blow. The science of hearing was still in its infancy and the specialists of the day asserted that a child with such a disability would not begin to speak, if at all, until she learned to read and master the art of sign language.

Princess Victoria refused to accept this counsel of despair. She heard of a German doctor who was teaching young children to lip-read so that their powers of communication were scarcely impaired and their deafness barely apparent in later life. She visited an orphanage at Margate and saw how his principles were brilliantly put into practice among poor and parentless children. But there were no similar group facilities for the deaf and speechless of well-to-do families, and no instructor could spare time for a single child, let alone the doubtful task of teaching an infant well below school age.

Princess Victoria decided that she would teach her daughter herself. Family influences were a contributory factor, for her own mother had died of diphtheria contracted while nursing her family, and now Princess Victoria was determined to leave nothing undone in freeing her own child from her imprisoning silence. She read every book she could find on deaf-mutism, filling notebooks with the factors that might influence her baby's development and self-expression.

On the other side of the world, though the Princess could not know it, a young woman named Anne Sullivan Macy was equally preparing herself for the far more difficult task of educating the blind-and-deaf Helen Keller, a triumph in which Princess Victoria took an intense interest when the story was told many years late. As an old lady, when living in Kensington Palace and known to the modern world as the Marchioness of Milford Haven, she seldom spoke of her own struggle. When her husband was posted to Malta and she presently joined him there, the other naval officer's wives thought of Princess Alice as a "quiet, pretty child", without knowing the inner story.

One of Princess Alice's earliest memories was of watching her mother's lips and linking her words with a picture-book but she was too young to remember the difficulties that were slowly overcome—not merely in moving her own lips in imitation but in learning the breathing, articulation and muscular control that most of us ordinarily take for granted.

It suffices that a childhood friend remembers playing at "housewives" with the Princess, sweeping the floor of a play cottage and pretending to bake cakes for tea, without being aware of more than "her slight deafness". And Prince Philip's cousin, Queen Alexandra of Yugoslavia, has recalled her own earliest impressions of her Aunt Alice "throwing out her words as if they were pellets, forming her phrases with a staccato emphasis that seemed to enrich them . . ."

Princess Alice's own childhood was, indeed, a progress of constant accomplishment. The summers were often spent in the gardens and woods around the white castle of Heiligenberg, the Hesse family estate which Prince Louis inherited. Then, in contrast, they lived for a time in a little house at Walton, where lessons were interspersed with excursions to see her great-grandmama, Queen Victoria, and to eat the revolting rice-puddings served with every nursery meal at Windsor Castle. Princess Alice was four years old when her sister, Louise, (later Queen of Sweden) was born, and her family nickname of "Shrimp" was surely to prove one of the more difficult words for Alice to enunciate. Her brother, George, arrived three years later; and the youngest of the family, Louis (today's Earl Mountbatten) was not born until 1900, when Princess Alice was already fifteen.

By then, Alice also learned to talk in both French and German and she went shortly afterwards to a finishing school in Darmstadt run by a stout redoubtable Fraulein Texter, where a younger friend, Meriel Buchanan, daughter of the British minister in Darmstadt, never quite forgot a schoolgirl crush on her.

"Princess Alice was my ideal, a paragon of perfection," she wrote long afterwards. "I wanted to copy her in all things, to be as tall and slender as she was, to hold myself with that grace and dignity that seemed to come to her naturally. . . . She was always at her ease, and never tongue-tied, self-conscious and awkward, as I so often was."

In her ardent eagerness to imitate the Princess, Meriel Buchanan even pretended to be hard of hearing at times, and she seemed unaware that her idol was, in fact, very shy. School friends were not the only ones to find a special fascination in the Princess's fair loveliness and in the "rather faraway look" that could so swiftly change to one of rapt attention. Among other visitors to Heiligenberg Castle at the time was a slim young soldier cadet who was youngest but one of the five sons of the Danish-born King George of Greece and happened to be only three years Alice's senior. Training with the Hessian 23rd Dragoons, stationed in Darmstadt, Prince Andrew was enchanted by the blonde and enigmatic girl who seemed to hang on his words with such unwavering intensity. At a birthday ball at the little court of Darmstadt, he swept her masterfully into a waltz, dancing to music she could not hear, and is said to have claimed every other dance on her card.

Princess Alice and Prince Andrew met again in London during the furore of family gaiety centred upon the coronation of King Edward VII and Prince Andrew's aunt, Queen Alexandra, and presently their friendship reached such intensity that when the young officer-cadet returned to Athens they promised to write to each other every day. A friend once found Princess Alice in tears because, she explained between sobs, she had not heard from Andrew for a week. Fearing he might have had an accident or found a new friend, she refused to be comforted at the prospect of any delay in the post, but next day was radiant because five letters from Andrew had all arrived at once.

After coming of age, Prince Andrew lost no time in approaching Prince Louis for permission to marry his daughter, and in June, 1903, he proposed to the Princess amid the roses in the gardens of Sopwell, St Albans, where the Battenbergs were living at the time. The engagement of Princess Alice and Prince Andrew, parents of Prince Philip, was officially announced a few days later.

To a whole generation of royalty, the autumn wedding of Princess Alice and Prince Andrew was to seem in retrospect the last great family reunion before the global blaze of two world wars. Not until our own modern royal weddings in Westminster Abbey was the regal spectacle and gaiety revived and in the toy-town atmosphere of Darmstadt the processions and receptions were indelibly

THE QUEEN'S TREASURES

The photographs of the Queen's porcelain, silver, bibelots, clocks and dolls are reproduced by gracious permission of H.M. The Queen.

(ABOVE) *Made by Josiah Wedgwood for King George III and Queen Charlotte, this tea-service is considered the oldest in the Queen's possession.*

(BELOW) *Bearing the crests of the five regiments of the Brigade of Guards, this modern Royal Worcester service is one of the Queen's favourites in regular use.*

The Queen's Cup: presented to the Queen and the Duke of Edinburgh on the occasion of their State Visit to the United States of America, 1957, to a glass design by George Thompson and engraving design by Bruce Moore . . . a superb example of Steuben crystal.

(STEUBEN)

The Merry-Go-Round Bowl: a wedding gift to the Queen from the President of the United States . . . a design in crystal by Sidney Waugh.

(STEUBEN)

(RIGHT) *The Queen's Plate. Characteristic of the Regency in detail and splendour, this piece by the highly gifted goldsmith, Paul Storr, still enhances the splendour of State Banquets.*

(BELOW) *Many of the Queen's choicest pieces were arranged for this unique photograph. At back a pair of light sconces by Paul Storr (1816) flank a Peruvian silver dish. The gold oval tray, centre, is by Philip Rundell (1821). The circular dish and ewer, right, are marked T.N.1595 and the oblong casket dates from Charles II. To the left is a table centrepiece by Paul Crespin (1741) and a sauce boat by Nicholas Sprimont (1743).*

A

Veneered in ivory and ebony, this cedarwood tea-caddy bears medallions of George III and Queen Charlotte.

B

Fashioned by Fabergé in rose quartz, with nodding head and hands, only three of these little figures are known in the world, owned by H.M. The Queen, the Aga Khan and Mr. Onassis.

C

Formerly in Queen Mary's collection, this mosaic Easter egg in platinum and gold was presented by the Czar Nicholas II to his Czarina in 1914 and contains portraits of their children.

D

Of onyx mounted with gold, a treasured toilet case is 200 years old and contains two scent bottles with stoppers of Chelsea porcelain in the form of birds.

E

With diamond dew-drops twinkling on its stalk, this actual size cherry in red enamel contains a diamond watch.

F

Encrusted with diamonds and mounted with gold, this bloodstock box was probably a gift of Frederick the Great to Catherine the Great of Russia.

G

A grand piano standing only 1½ inches high, wrought by Fabergé in Siberian jade with gold mounts.

B

THE QUEEN'S BIBELOTS

H

Inherited from Queen Mary, an early 19th-century Spanish fan bears a view of the Roya Palace in Madrid.

A

C

D

E

F

G

H

MEMENTOS OF TRAVEL

(RIGHT) *Presented to the Queen by the President of Federal Germany, a pair of crystal candlesticks mounted upon Wedgwood bases;* and (BELOW) *a silver bowl with a pattern of cornsheaves, designed by Prince Sigvard of Sweden (son of King Gustaf VI) and made in the Copenhagen workshops of Georg Jensen.*

Perhaps the finest and certainly one of the strangest clocks of the Queen's collection; the sunflower centred in the bouquet of Dresden china flowers is a clock with circling bees to tell the time.

(RIGHT) *'France' and 'Marianne' were favourite dolls of the Queen and Princess Margaret.* (BELOW) *Nearly 150 dolls of all nationalities are displayed at Windsor Castle.*

magnified into nearly a week of festivities. Emperors and Queens, Grand Dukes and Princesses converged from the four corners of Europe. Escorts of gleaming, jingling cavalry met every train, and the cavalcades of four-horsed carriages moved slowly through streets crowded day and night with spectators.

The Czar of Russia arrived with the Imperial Russian Choir, the King and Queen of Greece came with over thirty close relatives and the Grand Duke Ernest of Hesse imported a troupe of ballerinas for a gala performance in his theatre. Queen Alexandra brought an entourage of young English cousins. Princess Beatrice came with her daughter, Princess Ena, who was destined within two years to become Queen of Spain. Prince and Princess Louis welcomed their kith and kin to the preliminary reception in the ballroom of the Old Palace, a procession of beautiful women in magnificent tiaras and sequin-embroidered gowns and princes resplendent in Court uniforms and decorations.

There were in fact five wedding ceremonies, two of them rehearsals with youthful guests only, at Princess Alice's suggestion, so that all the children could enjoy a front view. On the wedding-day itself a simple Protestant service was first held in the castle chapel, then a civil ceremony under German law and finally the full splendour of a Greek Orthodox service surrounded the young couple at the Russian church, where Prince Andrew's four brothers held jewelled crowns, brought from Imperial Russia, over the heads of the bridal pair. Unable to lip-read through the dense beards of the three Orthodox Greek priests, Princess Alice answered "No" when asked if she consented to marry of her own free will and replied "Yes" when asked if she had promised her hand to anyone else, but no other mishap marred the complicated ritual.

Such was the marriage of Prince Philip's parents. The wedding breakfast was held in the great banqueting hall of the Palace and when the time came for the young couple to leave on their honeymoon at Heiligenberg, the fun grew fast and furious. Rice and confetti showered down as the bride and groom waved from their open carriage and, as it moved off, the guests gave chase, headed by the Czar, who raced across the courtyard in time to intercept the carriage at the corner and hurl a satin slipper at the bride. Princess

Alice caught it and expertly returned it like a boomerang, crowning the Czar of all the Russias with the heel and leaving him helpless with laughter in the middle of the street.

A residential suite in the Royal palace awaited the newly-weds in Athens. Like her mother, accustomed to changing house when following the Fleet, Princess Alice felt that she could make a home anywhere, but the first winter in the vast and old-fashioned palace turned out to be a daunting experience. The rooms prepared for her were filled with enormous pieces of heavy German furniture, darkened by heavy plush curtains and swept with icy draughts which the porcelain stoves were powerless to resist. The evenings were spent in semi-suffocation from the fumes and blue smoke of oil-lamps and, despite the optimistic efforts of a series of plumbers, the bathroom taps seldom gushed hot water.

It was a family joke that, when his sons were younger, the King used to lead his family in bicycle and roller-skating races through the Palace corridors to help them all to keep warm. Princess Alice brightened her apartments with chintz cushions but the replacement of the curtains needed the approval of a Palace bureaucracy which indefinitely postponed a decision until, with Mountbatten finesse, Princess Alice renewed the hangings at her own expense with hand-woven material from the School of Greek Embroidery, which effectively stilled all complaints.

Yet, if her surroundings were chilly and uncomfortable, the young British bride found herself in the midst of a large and warm-hearted family of tremendous verve and geniality. Once a week, when all the family lunched with the King, everyone seemed to talk at once in a patois of English, French, Danish and Russian, though Prince Andrew punctiliously insisted on speaking Greek in front of the servants. His elder brother Nicholas had married the Grand Duchess Helen of Russia only the previous year and Alice began learning Greek from her Russian-born sister-in-law, who enjoys a special place in British annals as the mother of Princess Marina. Princess Helen's first baby, Olga, was then only six months old. Another daughter, Elizabeth, was born in the following summer and, shortly after her christening, Princess Alice learned to her joy that she, too, was to have a child.

As a soldier, Prince Andrew probably hoped for a son, but a daughter, Margarita, was born to Princess Alice on 18 April, 1905, only a few weeks after the young mother's twentieth birthday. Princess Margarita is, of course, Prince Philip's eldest sister and sister-in-law to the Queen, though widely regarded today as one of the Royal Family's more obscure "German" relatives. But she arrived with considerable Mountbatten aplomb. Her grandfather, Prince Louis, received a telegram aboard the battleship *Drake*, where he was in command of the Second Cruiser Squadron on manoeuvres in the Mediterranean, and within a few days all six cruisers set sail for Greece. Pennanted to the topmasts, they dramatically sailed into the sunshine of Phaleron Bay on 8 May; and guards of honour of both British sailors and skirted Greek evones greeted guests to the baby's christening at the Royal Palace two days later. Among the godparents was Queen Alexandra, who had travelled from London some weeks earlier to join her brother, King George of Greece, in readiness for the event.

Admittedly, the birth of Princess Alice's second daughter, Princess Theodora, caused less fuss the following year. Then Princess Helen in turn had a daughter, Princess Marina. Indeed, the friendship of the two sisters-in-law, Helen and Alice, formed an interwoven chain of family events during the years leading up to the first world war. Both had summer homes in the secluded, pine-scented royal estate of Tatoi. Both families at times utilised the same English nurses, a Nanny Fox and a Nanny Roose, who relieved one another's duties during holidays. Soon there were six little girls, setting out with one another for their daily drives or picnic excursions to royal farms and ravines, with Princess Alice waving them goodbye from her world of silence. The two families enjoyed holidays together at the English seaside and shared the fantastic interludes when Princess Helen visited her mother in Russia in inimitable Czarist style.

The Czar's royal yacht transported them all through the Bosphorus and across the Black Sea to Sebastopol, and there they would find the luxurious imperial train awaiting them for the journey north to Tsarskoe Selo. Much had been made of the gilded spires, the rooms of amber and lapis lazuli, of the Czar's fabulous summer palace, but Helen's old home was in an excessively "Victorian" villa in the park, and camp beds had to be set up for the children. During one of these visits Princess Alice renewed acquaintance with her Aunt Ella, her mother's eldest sister, whose way of life was to make a deep impression upon her. As a Hesse princess, Ella had married the Grand Duke Serge of Russia and when he was assassinated she had given away all her personal possessions and joined the Sisterhood of Martha and Mary to devote herself to holy charity.

Princess Alice had been secretly shocked by the poverty she found in both Greece and Russia and had quickly interested herself, as we have seen, in the School of Greek Embroidery, with its philanthropic interest in teaching a craft from which the poorest women could gain an income in their own homes. Princess Alice herself learned the intricate stitches and subtle mingling of colours and instituted classes to help teach the art in small towns and suburbs. In 1912, when Greece was embroiled in the war with Turkey, Prince Andrew was called to his regiment and Princess Alice set up her own organisation to provide comforts for the men at the front, with a lively new approach which some royal ladies thought too advanced.

Impetuously she issued a notice "to all the women of Greece who will help me", announcing that she would be at the Royal Palace every afternoon from three to five to receive gifts. In today's setting, it would be rather as if someone as popular as Princess Alexandra had undertaken to receive all gifts in person. The queues of eager donors stretched down the street and Princess Alice tirelessly stood at her receiving desk, smiling her thanks, often until seven or eight o'clock in the evening. Then she invariably attended nursing classes and when the King visited the Salonika front, Princess Alice—still in her twenties—startled everyone by accompanying him in order to ensure that needed medical supplies efficiently reached the hospitals, crowded with wounded, near the front line.

Only a year later, the King was struck down by an assassin while walking in the streets of Athens, and Prince Andrew's nephew, Constantine, succeeded to the throne. Inevitably Princess Alice endured bitter anxiety for her own husband, with an intuitive sense that many tragic events were still to come. Before long, however, life seemed to resume a pleasant tenor and on 26 June, 1914, the Princess gave birth to her fourth daughter, Princess Sophie. Three days later she heard of the assassinations at Sarajevo that led to the first world war.

In all her darker fears for the future Princess Alice had not realised how decisively war would split her family assunder. Her twenty-one-year-old brother George was serving aboard the battle cruiser *New Zealand*, and she was suddenly cut off from news of Hesse cousins who were serving in the German army. Her younger brother, Louis (Earl Mountbatten) was urged forward in his studies as a cadet at Dartmouth Naval College in the intensive drive for new officers for the Royal Navy. As First Sea Lord, her father had sent out the signal for the British Fleet to commence hostilities against Germany and yet, within three months, at the very summit of his career, he was to be hounded out of the Navy in a fantastic and savage outcry against his German origin. As Princess Alice has recalled, with characteristic understatement, "When the rumours began, and the troubles, we all of us felt it very much."

While her brother-in-law, King Constantine, struggled to preserve Greek neutrality—all the more difficult in that his wife was German—the Princess's husband travelled between London and Paris in diplomatic endeavours to convince the Allied statesmen that the inexperienced King was not indulging in treacherous overtures to the Kaiser. Prince Andrew's efforts were all in vain. On a fine autumn afternoon in 1915, Princess Alice was working in the needlework shop at the School of Embroidery as usual when she felt the unmistakable vibration of an explosion, first one and then another, and from the window she saw that the people in the streets were wildly running for shelter. Then a colleague answered the telephone and reported that Allied warships were shelling the city.

A friend drove the Princess home at top speed, regardless of the falling shrapnel and rattle of rifle fire which, as they neared the Palace, grew more intense. The Palace itself was under fire from a shore party of French marines. Princess Alice had to skirt a barrier and rushed to her children's playroom to find the windows shattered and bullets embedded in the broken plaster of the wall. Her three elder daughters—aged five to ten—had been playing there at the time of the shots and yet had escaped unscathed. The nurses had rushed them down to the cellars with the baby and "Roosie' told them fairy stories until the firing ceased.

As Princess Alice said later, this one personal experience under fire was a small hardship to bear. But the Allies shortly afterwards recognised a new government in Greece and King Constantine had to relinquish his throne, to be succeeded by his son, Alexander. Both Prince Nicholas and Prince Andrew, with their families, had to follow their elder brother into exile. In June, 1917, Princess Alice was able to write to her younger sister, Louise, who was nursing in France, announcing their safe arrival in Geneva and within a few months she was permitted to visit England to be reunited with her parents, living in retirement on the Isle of Wight.

This was the summer when King George V ordered the abandonment of German princely titles and the Battenberg family name was changed to Mountbatten. Alice's father and mother were however created the Marquess and Marchioness of Milford Haven, a title which the younger generation were to find "a time-wasting style to have to write on an envelope".

Great changes often hinge on small events. In October, 1920, King Alexander of Greece died from the bite of a pet monkey, and his people decided by an overwhelming plebiscite that his father, Constantine, should return as King with all the former Royal Family. Princess Alice, then in her middle thirties, could hardly wait to see the land where all her four daughters had been born and when she discovered that she was to have another child, perhaps early in the following summer, her joy was complete. The Princess and her husband decided to waste no time but to return ahead of the King. "The children are beside themselves . . ." she wrote to her Battenberg Aunt Marie. "Everything abroad seemed to them grey and desolate: their young hearts sighed for the ever-blue sky and the hot sunshine."

On the death of his father, eight years earlier, Prince Andrew had inherited the villa and small estate of Mon Repos on the isle of Corfu. They had thought wistfully of its beauty and seclusion so often during their three years of exile: its dreaming garden of magnolia, eucalyptus, cypress and lemon trees, its steep paths winding down to the soft wavelets of the Ionian Sea. After their long absence Prince Andrew had feared that they might find it neglected and in decay, but the one or two household servants who remained had, as they promised, kept everything in order. When Princess Alice and the children ran down the broad sunny hall and through the French windows into the garden, it was even more beautiful in the sunshine than they perhaps remembered.

In the ardour of that homecoming, Prince Andrew was of course again full of hopes that the coming baby might prove to be a son and heir, and both he and his wife looked forward to at last leading a happy and settled life in their island home. Yet they had hardly settled in before a quarrel arose between Greece and Turkey and Prince Andrew was recalled to the Colours. Princess Alice had to content herself with reading his letters from the front while "Roosie" laid in a stock of British baby foods, saying enigmatically that it would need to be a vigorous child. June was a month of family birthdays and, on 10 June, Prince Andrew received a telegram announcing the arrival of a boy. His son was born sixth in succession to the Greek throne and christened, simply, "Philip" in the private chapel of the Royal Palace in Athens. Alice and Andrew had long since agreed that there was no need to burden their children with a string of names.

Convinced that the baby strongly resembled her husband, but with a Mountbatten look, too, Princess Alice longed to show this chubby boy to her parents and she was expectantly preparing her journey to England when her sister-in-law, Princess Helen, came to her to break the tragic and totally unexpected news from London that her father, the Marquess of Milford Haven, had suddenly died. Instead of the happy visit that she had anticipated, Alice hurried to England to be at her widowed mother's side, with "Roosie" and the baby.

They stayed at the house near Netley Abbey known as Fishponds, and friends presently sought to relieve the sad atmosphere by referring to Philip as "the dear little fish". (His Aunt Louise, the future Queen of Sweden, was after all still fondly known among her intimates as "Shrimp".) Fortunately, the nickname gained no favour and was quite forgotten the following year, under far brighter circumstances, when Princess Alice brought all her children to England for the marriage for her youngest brother, Lord Louis Mountbatten, to Edwina Ashley. The one-year-old Philip had then just reached the stage of taking his first few steps and so this might be propitiously regarded as the occasion when he first set foot on English soil.

His four sisters were bridesmaids in pale delphinium blue at their uncle's wedding at St Margaret's, Westminster, "A group of Tanagra figures", as old aunt Marie Battenberg affectionally recorded in her memoirs. In London, Princess Alice stayed for two or three weeks with her mother, now newly installed in a grace-and-favour suite in Kensington Palace and, among other royal visitors, Queen Alexandra, Queen Mary and Princess Mary came to admire her chubby fair-haired little boy.

Taking a fresh assessment of Princess Alice in her late thirties one of her relatives found her "the centre of her group of children, four charming girls and a boy", and on returning to Mon Repos, the Princess little knew that this was to be her last summer of enjoyment of that idyllic island home. Only a few months earlier her husband had considered that the campaign against Turkey was going well and might soon be brought to a victorious close. But now he was seriously alarmed at the follies that were being committed by the High Command and, when he received orders that he judged were impossible, he tendered his resignation. This was refused but leave of absence was granted and he joined his family at Mon Repos. In September, however, the Greek Army suffered disasters of such magnitude that King Constantine again had to relinquish the Throne, and Princess Alice discovered to her alarm that her own home was being watched by the police.

In the counter-revolutionary turmoil, six former members of the government were put on trial for their lives. Prince Andrew also was summoned to Athens on a pretext of being required to give evidence and when he failed to return home the Princess discovered that he, too, had been arrested.

Hurrying to Athens to do what she could, she seemed to face an iron curtain of delays and difficulties. Prince Andrew was held in solitary confinement, awaiting trial, and permitted to receive neither letters nor visitors. Alice rushed to Tatoi to plead with her nephew, the new King George II, but found that he in turn was practically a prisoner in his own house and powerless to help her. The air was charged with menace. Under interrogation at the tribunal headquarters, Prince Andrew was asked how many children he had and he answered that he had five. "Poor little things!" said his questioner. "What a pity they will so soon be orphans."

One by one the other accused men—including three ex-premiers and a former Cabinet—were sentenced to death. Prince Andrew knew that he would be next and by a smuggled message written on cigarette paper he indicated that he had given up hope. But it was evident that his accusers had reckoned without Princess Alice's own feminine share in the Mountbatten trait of tenacious determination. Like so many other deaf people, she had a compensating power of self-expression with her pen that now stood her in good stead. She wrote to her cousin, King George V, in England, desperately appealing to him to do what he could. She wrote to her Battenberg kinsman, King Alfonso of Spain, to President Poincare of France and to the Pope. She wrote to every royal relative throughout Europe and to every Allied statesman who might bring influence to bear, and her unremitting efforts succeeded in focussing the horrified attention of the civilised world.

Special envoys set out from London and Paris, Madrid and Rome, yet this was before the era of the passenger plane and they travelled at the usual diplomatic pace by rail and road. The British Minister in Athens reassured Princess Alice that the British cruiser *Calypso* was steaming towards Greek waters at full speed. But could help arrive in time? Meanwhile, the five condemned politicians were lined up in a prison courtyard and shot, without being allowed to see their families or permitted religious consolation.

The trial ended on a Saturday and the court retired without giving its verdict while Princess Alice endured a night of suspense.

She prayed desperately that her husband's life should be spared, and in the morning to her relief and joy she heard that Andrew had been sentenced to banishment from Greece. Within the hour, husband and wife were within the security of the British Legation and next day they sailed aboard the *Calypso*, safe and sound. The warship then called at Corfu to pick up the children and Miss Roose and, according to the family tale, Prince Philip was still so small that the sailors feared he might fall out of a bunk and padded an orange-box to form his cot.

Princess Alice's eldest daughter, Princess Margarita, can still remember that magical first Christmas at Kensington Palace and Sandringham. She was herself seventeen, full of the vivid impressions that come with that age, among them perhaps the memory of her father reprieved to a new lease of life and gay as a schoolboy, pretending to be a Christmas reindeer, monocle in his eye. Her Uncle Dickie and new Aunt Edwina—Lord and Lady Louis Mountbatten—invited them to see a comic film they had made with Charlie Chaplin in Hollywood during their honeymoon, and her mother heightened the family fun by lip-reading the silent film and telling them what the actors were really saying.

Not long before, Andrew's younger brother, Prince Christopher, had married a rich and attractive American widow, Mrs Nancy Leeds, and in the New Year of 1923 Alice and Andrew were invited to make "a jaunt of America" with all expenses paid. "Cristo" and Nancy would not hear of a refusal. The journey began in New York, with a side trip to Montreal, where delegations of welcoming Canadians presented so many bouquets to Princess Alice that she could scarcely carry them away. Then southward to Washington and Palm Beach, where they stayed at the fabulous Poinsiana, a vast and rambling hotel built so much in the spirit of the 1920's that the page-boys sped up and down the corridors on bicycles and breakfasts were delivered to the bedrooms by electrically-driven and heated trolleys.

That summer, in an attempt to repay Cristo's hospitality, Andrew rented a villa in Arcachon, the pretty spa near Bordeaux, where, as it turned out, nearly everybody came except Cristo! Alice's younger sister, Louise, arrived with the Crown Prince of Sweden, to whom she had announced her engagement shortly before and, at the wedding in the Chapel Royal, St James's Palace, Alice's daughters once again formed a quartet of bridesmaids, this time in apricot chiffon. A leisurely holiday was spent, too, in Monte Carlo, where another of Andrew's brothers, Prince George, had married Princess Marie Bonaparte, whose family had actually founded the famed casino and indeed still owned a great deal of property. This couple were instrumental in causing Alice and Andrew to settle in Paris, for Princess Marie claimed expansively that nine or ten could live cheaply as one and found space for the whole family in her huge mansion on the edge of the Bois. Then, a little later on, Alice and Andrew were offered a small lodge in her orchard at St Cloud, the house that Prince Philip recalls as one of the first homes of his boyhood.

Prince Andrew took great delight in all the sociable pleasures of Paris, but the constant invitations on their mantelshelf troubled Princess Alice, unable to resist the whispering of her conscience that his life had been spared for less frivolous purpose. As this inner conviction deepened, she started a national charity shop called "Hellas" on the Rue Faubourg St Honore to sell Greek embroideries, tapestries and art-work to help the many Greek refugees and exiles far worse off than themselves. She spent hours at its counters, coping with customers who seldom realized that she could not in fact hear a word they said. Young Philip, too, was deeply impressed in his own way and one day when he happened to see an Algerian carpet-seller at St Cloud, he rushed into the house and eagerly began offering his mother's own rugs for sale.

Prince Andrew will be chiefly remembered in history as the father of Prince Philip, but to a generation of nephews and nieces he remains a genial smiling figure, an uncle "full of inconsequential banter", although he could be "dogmatic and intense in patriotism and would sometimes talk to one very seriously". To younger members of the Swedish royal family, he is remembered as an uncle who would take them to the best *patisserie* in town and order a coffee, mysteriously smelling of cognac, while his youthful guests tucked into the creamiest pastries they had ever seen. To his teenage niece, subsequently Queen Alexandra of Yugoslavia, he was a solicitous host who would take her to Fouquet's restaurant "with a keen and zestful eye for human oddity . . . a connoisseur of the good things of life". Other young friends remembered him at St Moritz, snowballing them playfully but preferring to sit in the sunshine with a friend rather than try the ski slopes. Beside him at luncheon, Queen Alexandra noticed, there was "always a silver bucket of something on ice". Princess Alice, on the other hand, became more austere and sparing in her tastes in middle age, her deafness driving her ever deeper into a world of rapt contemplation and, when ill-health also dogged her, the growing disparity with her husband grew apparent. Prince Andrew could produce qualities of tenderness and "a gentle gravity", but he evinced, too, a sharp impatience at times and friends could resently foresee a breaking point when the girls were grown up, and Philip went away to school.

In 1931, in fact, all four daughters were married practically within the same year. Bridesmaids together, they were swept by an invincible fever to be brides together. The youngest and smallest of the family, Princess Sophie—"Tiny", as she was always known—came to her mother bright-eyed one day to tell of her fondness for tall Prince Christopher of Hesse. "But you are only sixteen—and he is thirty!" Princess Alice remonstrated, and yet at once saw the point of the age-old argument that age does not matter when one is in love. During the wedding preparations, Alice's third daughter—the nineteen-year-old Princess Cecile—met the Grand Duke George of Hesse, who was only five years her senior, and in February, just after Sophie returned from her honeymoon, they were married in Darmstadt.

Time had spun its full circle, and Princess Alice found herself again, surrounded with wedding festivities, at the scene of her own wedding. Two months later, her eldest daughter, Princess Margarita—then in her mid-twenties—married the tall, dark Prince Godfrey of Hohenlohe-Langenburg, whose family were descended from Queen Victoria's little-known half-sister, Feodora*. Then the

* *Queen Victoria's Sister* by Harold A. Albert.

summer of 1931 saw the wedding of Alice's second daughter, Princess Theodora, to Prince Berthold of Baden. Bride and bridegroom were precisely the same age and had much in common, especially their lively enthusiasm for new and liberal ideas in education. "Dolla", as Theodora was known to her friends, had always been the most serious and reserved of the four sisters, laughingly accusing herself of being inclined to the teaching profession and now she was marrying the son of the man who had founded one of the most progressive schools in the world.

This was, of course, Salem, which Prince Philip presently attended and Prince Max of Baden had first launched experimentally in a wing of his castle overlooking Lake Constance. Among the guests at the wedding was his former secretary, Kurt Hahn, who subsequently founded Gordonstoun, and so Dolla's "marriage of mind and heart" was to have an immense effect on the future.

All four brides wore Princess Alice's wedding veil, which her mother and grandmother had worn before her, but now it was again laid away in its lavender and tissue. With their four girls duly married and with Philip at Cheam prep school, safely in the care of his Mountbatten uncles, Alice and Andrew quietly elected to go their own ways.

When Princess Alice celebrated her fiftieth birthday in 1935, all her family conspired together to invite her on a round of continuous visits. She went to see her sister, Louise, then Crown Princess of Sweden, to rest and recuperate in her lakeside garden at Sofiero, ablaze just at that time with the blossoms of early Spring. She stayed with her eldest daughter and son-in-law, Margarita and Godfrey at Langenburg, where her room in the old castle overlooked the fragrant bowl of pinewoods threaded by the River Jagst, and flowers were always massed in her window. She paid a visit to her old friend, Princess Aspasia of Greece, devoted to her garden on a Venetian islet, and was overjoyed when Prince Andrew came to see her from Monte Carl. Then there was a stay at Salem with "Dolla" (Princess Theodora) and Berthold, whose baby daughter, another Princess Margarita, had first made Alice a grandmama in 1932.

At the age of twenty, Princess Sophie, the youngest of Prince Philip's sisters, was the mother of two little girls, while Alice's other—and perhaps favourite—daughter, Princess Cecile, by then had two boys. The families of his four sisters were, in fact, to make young Prince Philip an uncle thirteen times over while he was still a schoolboy, and all the sisters hoped that Princess Alice's health might be restored by affectionate involvement with the grandchildren whom she loved to see. To one of her close friends at this time, the Princess mentioned fears, premature though they might be, lest she should become a burden to others and her conflicting anxiety at the same time that she was still not doing enough for others. The family even watched her finances with some concern, aware of her inclination to dip far too redily into her purse, meeting the claims of a multitude of good causes more generously than she could afford.

Prince Philip had perhaps discovered his mother's approval of personal sacrfice as a small boy of only eight or nine when spending a seaside holiday with some family friends at Berck Plage. A beach acquaintance one afternoon bought all the children toys, but overlooked a gift for the little girl of the group—of those very existence indeed he was probably unaware—an invalid who was seldom able to leave her balcony. Philip promptly hurried away to her room with his gift toys and gave them all to her, a gesture rewarded with such unusual praise from his mother and others that he gathered up all the toys he had himself brought on holiday and rushed back to heap them around the invalid.

Princess Alice's niece, Queen Alexandra, was similarly impressed by her aunt's skill in compiling incredibly economical dishes, including an orange compote, boiled to bring out the flavour, which nevertheless meant more money to spare for her charities. At the back of the Princess's mind there still remained the haunting image of her favourite Aunt Ella.

As we have seen, her mother's eldest sister had married the Grand Duke Serge of Russia and, on being widowed by an assassin, had given everything she had to the poor and founded the only sisterhood of nursing in Russia. The young people were apt to be a little irreverent about her activities. "We stopped for Aunt Ella to go to church again," Princess Louise once wrote in her diary during a pre-war cruise on the Volga. "As she has now taken Holy Orders she naturally can hardly pass a town with a church without thinking she should go to a service." The Grand Duchess's saintly life caused her to be revered in Czarist Russia, a reputation which nevertheless did not prevent the Bolsheviks flinging her to her death down a disused mineshaft in 1918.

A requiem is still sung for her three times a year at a Russian convent on the Mount of Olives, and the memory of this good-doing deeply religious woman had remained with her niece Alice as a constant inspiration and a challenge. In 1936, a further plebiscite in favour of the monarchy meant that the Princess could return to Greece to resume her old interests among the poor and especially her old hobby-horse of promoting cottage employment with embroidery. Yet she felt with troubled heart that this was not enough.

Then in November, 1937, a terrible disaster shook the entire family. Her daughter, Cecile, was flying to London for a family wedding with her husband and two young sons and close Hesse relatives, and the aircraft crashed in flames. There were no survivors. To Princess Alice this was an overwhelming blow to her courage and resistance. Her husband and daughters did all they could to ease her grief until, as her old friend, Meriel Buchanan, has said, "some inner spiritual force seemed to give her back her strength and restored her serenity, her composure and her resignation".

All the following year, Princess Alice busied herself with her plans to found a small religious community, although she had no funds to build a hospital or church as her Aunt Ella had done and the Greek Orthodox Church was unhelpful. For a long time, despite her persistence and fervour, she progressed little farther than the home-made habit, grey and simple in design which hung in the wardrobe of the guest room she occupied at Tatoi and occasionally began to wear when on public duty. Then her thoughts turned to the possibilities of a children's orphanage and her brother-in-law, Prince George of Greece, suggested that, if she wished, she might use his own house in Athens.

With her elderly companion, Madame Socopol, Princess Alice

ran from room to room, enchanted. In her mind's eye, the stately reception-rooms blossomed as nurseries and clinics while the ornate bedrooms became airy dormitories. The practical plans for utilising and equipping the house bristled with difficulties, however, and were apparently still incomplete when the war began. For a year Greece enjoyed a transient neutrality before the troops of Germany's Axis partner, Italy, invaded her soil, and Princess Alice diverted much of her energies to the international Red Cross. Family communications had become increasingly difficult. The hostilities between Britain and Germany had sharply severed the loyalties of the Princess's own children. Her son, Prince Philip, was serving in the Royal Navy, while her son-in-law, Sophie's husband, Prince Christopher of Hesse, had joined the Nazi Air Force. (He was killed over Italy in 1944.) Her two other sons-in-law were nominally high-ranking German officers, and her brother, Lord Louis Mountbatten, commanded the British destroyer *Kelly*. When Mussolini opened hostilities and Italian bombers raided Athens, the Royal Family was supposed to gather together and take shelter in the cellars of the old palace. Alice was usually the last to arrive, often bringing in with her children rescued from the streets to share her comparative safety.

And then Philip suddenly appeared, on shore leave from the battleship *Valiant*, and astonishingly handsome in his lieutenant's uniform. When discretion required, mother and son had acquired a useful technique of conversing without exchanging a sound. Princess Alice would read her son's silently moving lips and it was perhaps in this way and at about this time that Philip first told his mother of his growing affection for Princess Elizabeth and his hopes that possibly one day they might marry. There were plans, too, for the Greek Royal Family to find sanctuary in South Africa if the position in Athens should become untenable. Philip attempted to persuade his mother to promise to join them, but she merely shook her head and said in her forceful way, "We will see!"

In the event, Princess Alice refused to leave. When the Germans were considered to be only a day from Athens, and an R.A.F. plane was delegated to fly the Royal Family to Crete, she pressed upon the travellers a series of parting gifts, including—for her niece Alexandra—a huge box of luxurious stationery embossed with the initial "A" and a crown. "It will be most useful," she urged, "So fortunate that our initials are the same!" Alexandra found it an impractical package to stow aboard a Sunderland flying boat.

Silence fell over Athens after the Germans moved in, though Alice was now able to get into touch with her daughters in Germany and wrote that she had not felt so well for years and was thoroughly busy nursing and looking after the poor. Her husband was cut off in southern France but news of him presently filtered through neutral Sweden. "He still lives on board the yacht *Davida* at Cannes, and says he is not hungry as he is a small eater," wrote her sister, Louise, from neutral Sweden. "Food conditions are near starving on the Riviera. But he is now cut off from outside news . . . the port authorities have confiscated his radio."

With these meagre messages, Princess Alice made herself content. The Germans, she found, did not molest her and a sentinel was presently taken away to other duties after "wasting his time" at her gate. Soon, in addition to working every day in the crowded hospitals, she took over the care of twenty young war orphans. But her task grew more difficult as the months went by. The horrors of the German occupation intensified, and minimal rations became non-existent. A hospital colleague tried to ensure that the Princess should receive extra Red Cross food parcels but a signature was required for each parcel and Princess Alice refused to sign for anything extra. In despair the friend bought her a few necessities on the black market but still had to cover her tracks so that the Princess never knew from where the food came.

When guerilla fighting increased in the city, gas, electricity and water were cut off, and a friend remembers seeing the Princess returning alone through the darkened streets with an empty bag. In her incessant hunt for food for her orphans, she had been out by herself, regardless of the risk of street snipers who fired on passers-by. Towards the end of the war, Mr Harold Macmillan was able to visit her from Cairo and reported that he found Princess Alice living "in humble, not to say somewhat squalid conditions . . ."

"She made very little complaint, but when I pressed her to know if there was anything we could do, she admitted that she and her old lady-in-waiting needed food. They had enough bread but no stores of any kind—no sugar, tea, coffee, rice or any tinned foods." Mr Macmillan was able to arrange for Army stores to be given to her but these in turn seemed to be passed on to others whom, Alice claimed, needed them more.

As that year of ordeal, 1944, drew to its close Princess Alice had to bear the hard news that her husband had died suddenly, in his armchair, in a villa that old friends had loaned him in Monte Carlo. Shortly afterwards, her niece Queen Alexandra of Yugoslavia considered it merciful when the regulations of the Greek Communists "finally ejected every member of the Royal Family" and forced the Princess to leave Greece. Even then however the Princess refused to accept British protection until she had made certain that her orphans would be in good hands.

Princess Alice returned home to England in time for the rejoicings of peace and the rapture of a series of family reunions. "I am afraid we should hardly recognize each other now, if we were to meet," she had written from Athens to a friend of her girlhood, but this sombre mood had no place in the post-war excitement. There was the happiness of again seeing her mother, the Dowager Marchioness of Milford Haven, an old lady now, but full of delightful talk and memories and future plans. There was even dear Pye, who had faithfully served the Marchioness as personal maid for more than fifty years, a firm rock of domestic life. They had remained living at Kensington Palace through most of the war "until the bombs broke our windows," as Pye said, and they were back again in the beloved rooms as soon as the shattered panes could be mended.

Among the first to welcome Alice was her sister-in-law, the widowed Marchioness Nada of Milford-Haven, and Nada's sister, Lady Zia Wernher, effervescent with ideas to put everything into post-war order at Luton Hoo. Then Princess Alice stayed with her niece, Princess Marina, the Duchess of Kent, at Coppins and so involved her affections in the affairs of the young Kent family. From south-east Asia, the Princess's brother "Dickie" (Earl Mountbatten) had suggested she should make herself at home at Broadlands and since part of the house was still an annexe to the Royal Southampton Hospital, the Princess indeed felt perfectly at home.

The patients thought that she was a member of the nursing staff, seeing her about the grounds in her grey costume with its coiffed grey-silk headdress. At Marlborough House, Queen Mary was still surrounded with packing cases, "gradually unpacking all my things," as she said, when Princess Alice went there to lunch. Queen Mary had not previously seen Alice's nun-like costume, although she had heard via the Crown Princess Louise of Sweden of her uncomplaining ordeal in wartime Athens. But above all the chief lunch-table topic, amid the flowers and the crystal and the fine porcelain, was of Princess Elizabeth and Prince Philip.

Nearly twenty years earlier, Alice and Louise had lunched with Queen Mary and King George V at Windsor Castle on the very day that Princess Elizabeth was born. The Queen had enquired after Alice's "little boy", and now the moving tapestry of life was bringing events to a wonderful fulfilment. "I fell in love at nineteen and it lasted for ever," Queen Mary had softly confided to her old friend, Lady Airlie. "I believe Elizabeth fell in love with Philip the first time he went down to Windsor . . ." And now, to Philip's mother in turn, Queen Mary could talk comfortably of the romance. She had knitted scarves and pullovers for Philip during the war and indeed had followed his wartime career with the closest interest. Now there were only the practical difficulties to be ironed out—the problem of Prince Philip's nationality was obvious, but Queen Mary and Princess Alice alike overlooked the fact that Prince Philip was still technically a member of the Greek Orthodox Church. The Archbishop of Canterbury eventually felt it his duty to point this out.

Princess Alice's first post-war visit to Buckingham Palace appears to have been deliberately deferred lest it should fan the flames of rumour and, instead, she was invited to visit the King and Queen (George VI and the present Queen Mother) at Royal Lodge, Windsor. She was horrified to see that one of the gate lodges was a heap of rubble, for few people realized that bombs had fallen so close to the King and Queen's private home. Princess Alice had last seen

Princess Elizabeth when still a child, very much under her governess's wing, and now she was charmed by a radiant young woman. They took to one another at once. When speaking, Princess Elizabeth always thoughtfully turned her face towards Princess Alice to enable her lips to be read, and she often impulsively took Alice's hand as they talked, "conveying so much reciprocal feeling", as one friend noted.

It afforded special pleasure to Princess Alice when, at her suggestion, "Lilibet" agreed to sponsor as her first godchild the infant son of King Peter and Queen Alexandra of Yugoslavia at his christening in Westminster Abbey. The baby had been born at Claridge's and Alice was one of the young mother's first visitors "in the full flow of one of her talking moods," as Queen Alexandra noted "talking to me for hours on more aspects of baby care than I had ever imagined". In the tender imprint of the baby's features the Princess could detect a resemblance to her own lost daughter Cecile, and Alexander—as the baby was named—had also been the name of Cecile's own younger son who had perished with his mother in the air crash.

And so the tapestry was new-woven. Complaining that she could ill spare the time, Princess Alice was persuaded to take a short holiday on the west coast of Ireland, where the Mountbattens had a seaside home, and the sunshine and wonderful food restored colour and contour to cheeks tightened by wartime starvation. Another happiness, a few months later, was in the wedding at Romsey Abbey of Dickie's elder daughter, Patricia, to young Lord Brabourne, who had been on Earl Mountbatten's staff in south-east Asia. The reception at Broadlands seemed to be a vast pageant of old friends and, for all the passing of time, Patricia in her wedding-gown reminded many of Margarita as a bride, so striking was the family likeness.

This wedding marked the occasion when Prince Philip and Princess Elizabeth were first seen together in public, and Princess Alice knew it would be their turn next, despite the many questions still waiting to be settled. One of the special difficulties that troubled Philip was the problem of the engagement ring, and he blushed when he spoke of it. There were already such wonderful jewels in Princess Elizabeth's family: what could he possibly select that would be fittingly good enough, and how could he possible make a discreet choice when the newspapers were already watching his every step?

His mother was perhaps touched to find that he had been saving up from his naval pay for the ring: putting money aside so strenuously indeed that some of his brother officers considered him "stingy". Princess Alice had long since sacrificed most of her own jewels to philanthropy, and the chief exceptions were her engagement ring and a ring of diamonds that had belonged to her grandmother. Prince Philip, at all events, was told that his worries could be readily solved, for sentiment is part of the intrinsic value of the ring, and on his next leave his mother showed him some designs that she had herself sketched on paper.

Every jeweller in the land would have eagerly sought the honour of making Princess Elizabeth's engagement-ring but Princess Alice kept her own counsel. One afternoon, a "sister in grey" stepped out of the lift to the fourth-floor showroom of a discreet Bond Street jeweller and, producing a ring, the Princess asked if the stones could be reset to her own design. Although there were practical difficulties in her original pattern, the jeweller presently called at Kensington Palace with designs closely matching her wishes and embodying a solitaire diamond supported by diamond shoulders set in platinum. From first to last no one knew the ring was for Princess Elizabeth until after her betrothal, when the band had to be slightly reduced in size.

At the wedding Princess Alice wore a sweeping lace gown with a plumed toque and "processed" magnificently with Queen Mary down the nave of Westminster Abbey, but she insisted on keeping out of camera range in most of the private wedding pictures and was content to watch from the Chinese Room when the bride and groom and the Royal Family appeared to the cheering crowds on the Palace balcony.

The only shadow was that her three daughters, Margarita, "Dolla" (Theodora) and "Tiny" (Sophie) had not been invited to share this moment. The King's advisers had suggested that the presence of "German" princesses would be inopportune so soon after the war and the King deemed it incumbent upon him to accept their guidance. The story that one of the sisters came incognito as a private guest is quite untrue. All three, in fact, gathered to hear the broadcast of the wedding at Marienburg Castle, south of Hanover, the family home of Sophie's second husband, Prince George of Hanover. They did not know till later that Philip insisted on signing the wedding register with their joint wedding-gift, a gold fountain-pen engraved with their names, which he still uses on formal occasions to this day.

Marienburg itself, indeed, was closer in spirit to England than anyone realized at the time. The widowed Sophie had first met Prince George when visiting "Dolla" at Salem, where he was the school bursar and business manager. Descended from George III, he was also in fact a Prince of Great Britain and Ireland, a point subsequently thoroughly tested when his elder brother, Prince Ernest Augustus, took the question through the law-courts and the Court of Appeal in London finally decided that he was entitled to British nationality. The issue thoroughly amused and interested Princess Alice, who knew the intricacies of every family relationship. "If you want to know anything about the family, you must ask Mother," Prince Philip would often say. And in humorous mood Princess Alice would point out that since George of Hanover's sister was also her niece, Queen Frederika, the Queen of Greece might be legally a British national. It was indeed "all very complicated".

In any event, the absurd affront to Prince Philip's sisters met with the disapproval of the British public and was soon remedied. Dolla's son, Max, was a pupil at Gordonstoun; and Philip and Elizabeth had been married less than a year when, under the pretext of visiting young Prince Max, Dolla and her husband were guests at Balmoral. Princess Alice saw with pleasure that Prince Philip was taking a measured place in the family complex, and she impatiently brushed aside the assumption that there might be diplomatic obstacles. "It is all nonsense," she would say, "and we must get rid of it."

Lapped by the blue water of the Aegean Sea, shimmering under blue Grecian skies, the isle of Tinos is a place of ancient religious significance where the maimed and sick come in their thousands every August in a pilgrimage akin to Lourdes. Here in 1948 a life-long dream was briefly set in perspective for Princess Alice when she inaugurated a new community of Martha and Mary. Small acts of faith may found great enterprises in time, but the illustrated magazines of Europe visualised a large and ready-made organised community, complete with its chapel and cloister and well-staffed hospital and the journalists who descended on Tinos—enduring the occasionally rough sea passage—discovered this to be only a mirage. Burdened with cameras, a photographer was directed up a cobbled alley to a square, white, tiny two-floored house where, on asking for Princess Alice, a "nun in grey" at a washtub merely shook her head and went on with her task. There were, in fact, only two so-called nuns, the Princess and her younger companion, Sophie Alberti. Princess Alice had earnestly believed that if she began to work on the island for the sick and poor, the example would create its own sequel. Instead, only reporters besieged her. One beguiling visitor suggested that publicity would help to serve her cause. "I don't approve of publicity," replied the Princess. "Our work is sufficient in itself. And taking pictures of me at work would be posing."

Ultimately the interest of the press ebbed away, although newspapers continued for years to describe Princess Alice as the Mother Superior of a religious order on Tinos. In reality, the experiment was short-lived, if not a failure. The great pilgrimage to Tinos centres upon 15 August, when thousands bring their own mattresses and household paraphernalia and sleep on the floor of the church or under the stars of the courtyard. For a night or so, two of the Princess's rooms were similarly crowded with supplicants, while she retired with her companion to the third room. Yet she was left unsatisfied. The fishing and souvenir-selling population of Tinos offered insufficient scope for her energies; the priests were evidently unco-operative, and, during a visit to Athens, Earl Mountbatten did not have great difficulty persuading his sister that more useful activities might flow from establishing a working group closer to Athens. And so it proved.

A small villa in its own grounds was found in the suburb of Neon

Heraklion and organised with the help of an old friend of professional nursing experience as a combined convalescent home and nursing training school. If in retrospect we may suspect an indulgent family plan to keep Princess Alice happily and contentedly occupied in following her own chosen courses, the enterprise at least succeeded at every level. The nursing sisterhood lacked the melodramatic quality that had attracted the unwanted attentions of photographers and reporters to the isle of Tinos. One young member of the family could talk comfortably of "Aunt Alice and her old dears", but the Princess drew around herself several elderly gentlewomen of like mind who could all purposefully do a great deal of good.

When Prince Charles was born, for instance, hundreds of unforeseen gift parcels deluged Clarence House and the nursery staff coped with far more baby garments than an entire family of children could ever wear. Although the surplus was distributed to hospitals, a proportion was set aside for "Mama's charities". Nor was the sisterhood an institution of sleepy old-fashioned religious philanthropy. Prince Philip had given his mother a car. She had learned to drive in Switzerland many years before, proving that her keen eyesight and immunity from traffic noise unexpectedly heightened her ability at the wheel. In contrast with her wartime trudges, a friend tells a hilarious tale of seeing the Princess, her car stacked with parcels, driving like an angel possessed through the maelstrom of Athens traffic in Omonia Square.

Princess Alice had probably discovered that her son was a hoarder. He had trunks crammed with what his valet, John Dean, called "junk from childhood and schooldays, even baby clothes" which he firmly refused to empty. On one occasion, Dean suggested parting with these treasures but Philip firmly refused. "Certainly not" he said. "They are valuable and may be useful one day." When neither Prince Charles or Princess Anne used these heirlooms, however, the collection was weeded out, it seems, and consigned mainly to Athens. Perhaps Princess Alice put in a persuasive word.

Travelling as usual with only one suitcase, she visited London for the advent of Princess Elizabeth's second baby, and was on hand at Kensington Palace when Philip sent the message, "It's the sweetest girl". The baby was named Anne Elizabeth Alice Louise, and both Princess Alice and Princess Margarita were god-mothers. Philip's sister came to London for the christening but his mother preferred to hurry home to Athens, and Princess Alice of Athlone stood in as deputy sponsor in the ceremony at Buckingham Palace.

A notable milestone of family life also marked the following year when Philip and his wife spent what was supposed to be a private holiday in Greece, and their visit was inaugurated with a wonderful lunch party at Tatoi. The people of Greece however unmistakably wished to see more of the Princess. The streets blossomed with decorations, a visit to the City Hall became a State drive and Princess Alice found crowds of local folk waiting at her gate in the hope of catching a glimpse of her daughter-in-law.

Yet Princess Alice had seldom been so happy. Her son's intense popularity, with that of his wife, filled her with maternal joy and thankfulness. The young couple had come to Athens after spending Christmas in Malta and the future seemed to promise many such visits. But within the year the tragic death of King George VI and the accession of Elizabeth as Queen changed everything.

The sorrowful news had reached Princess Alice at midday and she spent most of the afternoon writing letters, among them a letter to Philip no doubt bidding him to faith and courage. Princess Alice was evidently counselled not to go to London. It did not immediately occur to that she was now mother-in-law of the Queen; and that she would never intrude on the public scene in that role went without saying. She prayed for guidance and quietly affirmed to her friend, Madame Valaoriti, her resolve to help the "Family" privately to the limit of her strength.

An early anxiety was that Philip fell ill under the strain and developed jaundice, an infection he had not had since a boy. That autumn Princess Alice also unavoidably worried when, as an indispensable ingredient of his modern royal duties, Prince Philip began learning to fly. Perhaps Louise—who had become Queen of Sweden in 1950—eased these misgivings by reminding her sister of the time when she (Louise) and Dickie—aged only six—had been safely up in a blimp airship back in 1906, in the true pioneering age of the air. The Princess was soon as airminded as anyone and before long, after staying at Balmoral, it became an everyday matter for her son to pilot her in one of the small royal aircraft from Dyce airfield to Prestwick to catch an airlines plane to Stockholm.

A wit has said that Prince Philip got his wings before the Queen got her crown. Early in 1953, he literally paid a (piloted) flying visit to his mother and sisters at Salem to round off family plans for the Coronation. Princess Alice has a gift for simplifying everything and in all the subsequent feminine discussion of clothes and jewels, she made everyone laugh by saying comfortably, "I shall buy myself a new grey dress".

When one is older, time itself flies faster. Looking back, Prince Philip's mother can scarcely believe that so many years have already passed since the Coronation. Staying at Buckingham Palace for the royal week of festivities were Queen Juliana of the Netherlands and Prince Bernhard, Crown Prince and Princess Olaf of Norway, Prince and Princess Axel of Denmark and Princess Alice with her three daughters and their husbands. It was the first time they had all been in London together. In her own tranquil rooms in Buckingham Palace today, Prince Philip's mother can look back at all the bustle and laughter, and the gaiety of that week of weeks merges in retrospect with the pleasure of a score of subsequent family visits to the Palace and the happiness of innumerable holidays at Balmoral.

In 1955, when Princess Alice celebrated her seventieth birthday, Prince Philip and Earl Mountbatten flew to Salem for her birthday party and, after the cutting of the cake, at least twelve of her present-day total of twenty grand-children gleefully helped to blow out the candles. Several great-grandchildren were also present, representative of the eight or nine of a recent listing of the very youngest generation.

Like all grannies, the Princess finds it difficult to keep count and claims fondly that her huge family makes her feel like Queen Victoria. Prince Charles and Princess Anne were too young to make the journey to Salem in 1955 but their grandmother joined them that summer on the cruise of the royal yacht *Britannia* to Wales, the Isle of Man and Scotland. Pacing the decks made her feel like a girl again, so vivid were the memories of the youthful days with her father in Malta. Princess Alice figured also in the picnic party ashore when Prince Charles first set foot in his future Principality, creating what historians might regard as a new link of historic interest with the Marquess of Milford Haven.

The Prince of Wales has always been extremely fond of his Mountbatten grandmother. An early memory is of the two of them sitting in a little caravan in the grounds of Buckingham Palace while she told him Bible stories that gained in excitement from her own emphasis in narration. When Charles was ten and had to be isolated with chicken-pox, his mother and sister could not go near him but his grandmother flew from Germany to keep him company, remarking that her isolation would trouble no one. Today the Prince of Wales writes to his grandmother wherever he is, letters that I am told are full of his own humour and more than a share of his mother's compassion.

In her seventy-fifth year it was a source of special pleasure to Princess Alice to meet him at Athens airport and welcome him to Greece—with Princess Anne, Princess Alexandra and others—when they came for the wedding of King Constantine to Princess Anne-Marie of Denmark. Charles and Anne stayed at Tatoi, and their grandmother rounded off her happiness by acting as a guide in the royal domains on two or three occasions when they went out sightseeing. With the mounting years, the time had come, she had decided, to relinquish her philanthropic and nursing work to others, leaving her more time for happiness with the family. When visiting London her presence was always unobtrusive and she could go shopping in Oxford Street quite unrecognized, vigorously walking home afterwards. With her sister, she once went shopping in Knightsbridge, assuring Queen Louise that they would be quite incognito. This was not quite the case, for the Queen of Sweden quickly attracted stares, though scarcely anyone glanced at her grey-clad companion.

Queen Louise extracted a promise from Princess Alice to spend her eightieth birthday with the King and herself in Stockholm and in 1965, under providence, they were thus together during the quiet February days at Drottningholm. All about them felt this to be a period of grace, for Queen Louise had already incurred two severe heart attacks and she died only ten days later. Oddly enough, the younger members of the family were making preparations at the time for the wedding of Princess Margarita's son, Prince Kraft, to Princess Charlotte de Croy and the ceremony was postponed. Shadows and sunshine, crisis and calm are all threaded in the fabric of life.

The wedding was deferred, indeed, until after the State visit to Germany of Prince Philip and the Queen. For the first time, Elizabeth saw all the family homes and her mother-in-law was content to watch from a fireside seat rather than take part in the glittering events that filled the Federal Republic with such excitement. Princess Alice's health was proving troublesome, even in summer, and after a period in hospital she fell in with the family persuasions that the time had come to enjoy the warm and air-conditioned apartments prepared for her in Buckingham Palace.

All the family constantly come to see her, and after the storms, the changes, the setbacks, it has been a true coming home. All around the Princess is the royal atmosphere in which she was born. Each day her morning tray is brought to her with its token nosegay of flowers and inviting pile of family letters. In the heart of London, under her son's roof, in her native land, Princess Alice has found sanctuary and serene anchorage.

THE POMP

9 A Secret History of the Coronation

The Coronation of Queen Elizabeth II was the widest-watched pageant—and probably the most deeply-felt religious service—ever held. Yet the record of what went on behind the scenes needs a new assessment.

For those old enough to remember, the year 1953 will always shine in the memory, for it was the year of the Coronation. Private joys and sorrows were submerged in the excitement of public rejoicing, though why the tug of emotion should be so real, why the gaiety and pleasure so infectious and genuine is something that only a serious student of the primeval urges of monarchy might find need to explain. The very year was auspicious as the nation emerged from the six years of war and the eight years of austerity into, at last, unfettered and long-sought normality. The emotion was real, not produced by platform histrionics or worked up by television trumpets and drums, and at its heart was the nascent figure of a young and beautiful woman, for the new Queen Elizabeth II was only twenty-seven.

The nation was in a mood of renaissance, talking of a new Elizabethan age. In the ferment of anticipation, not a street or alley in the land was without its decorations. In central London, everyone with a window over-looking the five-miles Coronation procession route had a realisable fortune in prospect, and seat ticket agents discovered there was no show business like the Coronation. You could chart the fever by the profiteering—£3,500 for a side-street balcony with champagne for fifty, £65 a seat for a view through the trees from Park Lane. And half-a-million people began camping free two days beforehand on the pavements.

They brought into the heart of London old mattresses last used in air-raid shelters in the blitz and they slept in their hundreds under the silvery trellis arches that decked the length of the Mall. They sang outside Buckingham Palace all the previous weekend and cheered the workmen still arriving for last-minute touches at Westminster Abbey.

After the lean years of post-war privation, everyone expected an unsurpassable pageant of dedication and rejoicing, and yet in reality the preparations moved forward on a floodtide of muddle.

The uncrowned Queen had reigned for over three months when the Coronation executive committee of twenty key men of the Establishment first met at St James's Palace. Grey-haired and elderly, they ranged from the Archbishop of Canterbury to the 75-year-old Lord Chamberlain, the Earl of Clarendon, and it must be said that many of their early decisions subsequently proved to be mistaken. They first fixed 2 June as the Coronation day, chiefly by taking the "safe" middle date between the coronations of George VI (12 May) and George V (22 June). Cries of dismay instantly rose from the tourist and hotel industry, for the extra crush and confusion would fall in Derby week, normally the busiest, fully-booked week of the year. Next, the Establishment elders decided that no part of the Coronation service should be televised, and a storm of anger broke. The people, it was said, were being deprived of the spectacle of a lifetime. But what was more evident was that the ban would deny the Queen's subjects the vivid sense of participation and kinship that the broadcasting of royal weddings and other events had evolved almost as a public prerogative.

Eighty M.P.'s tabled a motion of disapproval of the ban, but no one realized that the typed draft decision had travelled across court and government desks for four months without adverse comment. Even Mr Clement Attlee, that master of detail, admitted to having seen the document . . . without noticing the decision. The then Mr Winston Churchill disclaimed responsibility, although he and eight Cabinet Ministers sat on the committee. To heighten the disconcerting effect, both Churchill and Attlee sat on the larger Coronation Commission. And then to cap all, the elderly planners wished the route of the Coronation drive to be short, shorter even than that of George VI. But this was an idea that the Queen herself emphatically rejected. She insisted that thousands of extra schoolchildren

Princess Alice of Greece.
(See PRINCE PHILIP'S MOTHER)

(TOPIX)

The Queen at her desk.
(See THE QUEEN'S MAIL)

could get a view if the procession route were extended, and so the approved route was one of the longest on record.

When the Coronation ceremony itself came under scrutiny, her advisers wished to omit parts of the long and tiring three-hour ritual. The Queen merely asked, "Did my father do it?" and invariably added, "Then I will!"

In all these stories, one inevitably finds, nearly twenty years later, more than an echo of the sentiment and charm of the young Queen Victoria. A relative has told how, at Windsor, the new Queen Elizabeth noticed the first estate milk-bottles with her cypher "E.R. II" . . . and gleefully exclaimed that she had not felt like a Queen until that moment.

When her first postage stamps were being printed at a High Wycombe factory, the Queen motored out, anxious to see the first sheets as they came off the press.

Traditionally, the chief Coronation organiser was the Duke of Norfolk who, like his forebears for 500 years, earns £10 every six months for his hereditary duties as Earl Marshal. The Duke had handled George VI's Coronation when still in his inexperienced twenties, outwardly diffident, as Archbishop Lang thought him, but blending ancestral toughness with a courtier's tact. Although a Roman Catholic, he had even demanded the keys of the Abbey on security grounds and so incisive were his powers of persuasion that 60 bunches of keys were surrendered to a police officer, and the Dean and Chapter found themselves locked out of their own mother church.

In commencing the complex management of the 1953 Coronation, the Duke, then in his mid-forties, was fortified by a huge blue-bound encyclopaedia of the 1937 arrangements. It conveniently happened that the government had requisitioned a Norfolk ducal town house in Belgrave Square and leased it to NATO, but now NATO had quit the premises and the Duke of Norfolk in his guise as Earl Marshal moved in. A quiet room at the back became his ground floor office, and doors that had known smart dinner-parties, and then military secrets, assumed new labels. "Reception,

Dress . . ." "Clarenceux King of Arms" "Windsor Herald". The Coronation preparations began with the clatter of busy typewriters and the buzz of an intercom.

At an early stage the Duke signed a warrant authorising the Ministry of Work to commence work at the Abbey. His 1937 master book contained everything from architects' drawings for the street stands to sample invitation cards and plans for safeguarding the Crown Jewels, but the Earl Marshal could no longer rely on the 16-year-old formulas. They were a patternbook only. History supplied no satisfactory precedent, for example, for the part the Duke of Edinburgh would play as the Queen's consort.

The last married Queen Regnant had been carried in a chair to her crowning and her husband's only role had been to walk ahead of the procession of nobles. Prince Philip was chairman of the Coronation Commission. Even his precedence, in place next to the Queen, was not made clear however until the Queen signed a warrant to the effect when her reign was six months old. Should Prince Philip ride with the Queen in her coach or on horseback beside it or perhaps behind it? Should he sit apart in the Abbey in a Chair of State? What supporting role should be found for him in the religious ceremonial? Only the Queen herself could solve these problems, and among the alternatives submitted to her, she alone decided that Prince Philip should kneel before her bareheaded in homage as the first of the Royal Dukes and kneel beside her as her husband, when she had put off the Crown, in the private sacrament of Communion.

Again, the varied changes in the Commonwealth scene—the division of Ireland, the break-up of the Empire of India, the self-government of so many former colonies, all rendered revisions in the service imperative. Some of the changes in procedure were the first since 1689. Scotsmen felt a new wind stirring when they heard that the Moderator of the Assembly of the Church of Scotland was to take part in the ceremony for the first time, presenting the Bible jointly with the Archbishop of Canterbury. Sir Owen Morshead, the royal librarian, was asked for records of former crownings, including commentaries privately written by the central figures. Acquiescent in tradition, obedient to the Church, attentive to her advisers, the new Queen studied these until she became nearly as knowledgeable as the experts. Technically, the Dean of Westminster, Dr Dod, had the right of instructing the Queen in the "solemnities and meaning" of her installation, and perhaps an oversight occurred. Dr Dod was not summoned for "instruction" until a month beforehand, and he then found his pupil as thoroughly versed in the rubric and ritual as he was himself.

What was the Queen's own view of her Coronation? She regarded it as a consecration, a making of vows to her peoples, more than a crowning. Her demeanour at the ceremony was to disclose how fervent, how sincere, was that simple and personal act of faith. Within the ceremonial, notwithstanding, the Queen would omit no symbol that gave meaning to the rich pageantry and pomp, and she clearly sought to implant details of personal individuality.

Thus a minor dilemma arose when she declined to wear Queen Victoria's ring and General Sitwell, Keeper of the Jewel House, was told that the small circlet specially made for Queen Victoria's investment would not be required. Instead Elizabeth II elected to wear the masculine ring first made for William IV and since worn by every King, with its great sapphire and ruby Cross of St George. Her decision moreover embodied commonsense, for the feminine ring was too small even for Victoria's tiny hand, while jewellers readily reduced the man's ring in size.

All through the autumn of 1952 and the following spring millions of words of diplomatic text shuttled back and forth between Whitehall and the Commonwealth governments, St James's Palace and the Earl Marshal's sanctum in Belgrave Square. "I have it in command from The Queen . . ." "The Queen has decided . . ." The stream of official letters settled the problems one by one.

The Queen was reminded that armills or bracelets formed a part of the Regalia peculiarly suitable for a woman, though neglected since the time of Edward VI. Enquiries were instituted to see whether these half-forgotten tokens of sincerity and wisdom could be restored to a ritual, and Prime Minister Menzies of Australia brilliantly suggested a new pair of gold bracelets jointly contributed by the Commonwealth countries.

Commonwealth composers also contributed music for the first time. The Homage was by a Canadian and, at the Queen's direct wish, more new music and revised musical arrangements were embodied in the Service than in any previous Coronation.

The great TV controversy admittedly lasted longer than most. Archbishop Fisher and Winston Churchill were alike reluctant lest an act of worship became a theatrical peepshow. Public opinion was not mollified when Mr Churchill announced a compromise decision to televise the processions west of the Abbey screen. Happily, the Queen exerted her own feminine influence in discovering a solution. Just as her father welcomed the filming of his Coronation to enable it to be shared and understood to the fullest extent by his peoples, so the young Queen realised the immediate link of TV, although even she did not foresee its phenomenal impact. Her Majesty ultimately smoothed away the last difficulties during a lunch-table discussion with the Archbishop at Buckingham Palace, and the B.B.C. producers who had vainly pressed for so long for facilities were now astonished at the trouble taken to help them.

In reality, a more insidious risk to a modern monarchy lay in a curious trial of prerogatives held by old custom in the Privy Council chamber in Downing Street. For seven hundred years a Court of Claims has sat before every Coronation to decide who has the right to perform special services at the enthronement of the Sovereign, and in 1936 so many characters pressed forward with eccentric claims that the pomp and privilege threatened to dissolve in gales of laughter. Hereditary poulterers, waferers, herb-strewers and would-be rightful Stewards of England raised doubts and disputes that caused the court to discuss much of its business in whispers. In 1953 the Court erected a neat rabbit fence across the warren of medieval rules by first sitting in private and ruling that any claim excluded in 1936 could not be heard again.

Ample problems nevertheless remained to be settled. Who should be allowed to present a glove for the Queen's right hand—or to carry the canopy over her head? Who should be privileged to carry the Great Spurs or to bear the Crystal Mace? Who should support the Queen's right arm in carrying the Sceptre?

It was established that those with claims granted sixteen years earlier had but to say so in writing to retain the privilege. This mitigation saw the letter of feudal law scrupulously observed with minimum publicity. It seemed unlikely that four peers would fiercely contend for the right to bring their Sovereign's shirt and stockings on her Coronation morn, as they had in the reign of Edward VII. Nothing more was similarly heard of an 80-year-old Kentish old age pensioner who claimed a High Steward's right to carry the Crown. A Norfolk lady claimed that the tenure of Heydon Hall gave the right to carry a towel for the Queen, and the law lords effaced her privilege by making "no order".

More robust claims, speedily granted, however, saw the Clerk of the Crown allowed five yards of scarlet cloth as his fee, while the Dean and Chapter gained the Abbey fittings and ornament as their little-known perquisite.

Probably the most disappointed claimant was the Duke of Somerset who asked the right to bear the Orb or the Sceptre with the Cross, as his ancestors had done at nine coronations. The verdict went against him for lack of sufficient documentary evidence, though without prejudice to any hopes he might have of "an act of grace". The coveted tasks were nevertheless assigned elsewhere: the Lord Portal carried the Sceptre with the Cross in the grand procession preceding the Coronation while the Orb was borne by the popular Earl Alexander of Tunis.

The Duke of Newcastle equally saw his claim of ancestral rights dismissed on an unforeseen technicality. As lord of the manor of Worksop the Duke had the traditional right of presenting a glove for the Queen to wear while carrying the Sceptre and of placing the richly decorated glove upon her hand.

Immediately before the act of Crowning, the ceremonial had always paused for this special privilege. Dukes of Newcastle had enacted their role at the Coronations of Edward VII, George V and George VI. But now a new duke had to disclose that a limited company had been formed to look after his estates, and so the London and Fort George Land Company applied for its place of honour beside the Throne.

The chairman of the board, it was argued, could present the glove. A director of the company might support the Queen's arm.

After retiring to discuss this takeover bid in private, the law lords rejected the firm's claim without hope of appeal. Ultimately, the honour of presenting the glove was conferred upon the popular Lord Woolton, and the perfection of detail marking every part of the ceremonial demonstrated in the glove itself, of white kid, lined with white silk, the Royal Cipher on the back, the gauntlet embroidered with the rose, thistle and shamrock. In contrast to the disappearance of the Duke of Newcastle, others were startled at finding themselves in the midst of the proceedings at all. A Welsh schoolmaster's son, a certain Nigel Rees, headed the passing-out list on the officer-cadet training cruiser H.M.S. *Devonshire* and Prince Philip, impressed by his demeanour during a presentation, unexpectedly asked if he would like to be his page at the Coronation. The young man gasped his thanks.

Yet few actually took part in the ceremonies, they were officially reminded, save as a mark of Her Majesty's favour and esteem. Despite the reticence of the intensive undercover organisation surrounding her, it became widely known that Her Majesty had studied the appointment lists with extraordinary care. Ultimately everyone present in the Abbey was there because the Queen wished it.

Apart from personnel, a specific problem also lingered in the ingredients of the oil with which the Queen was to be anointed. The pale golden oil of the original base blended for Queen Victoria had been jealously preserved for use at each successive Coronation for more than a century, but the last phial was shattered when the Abbey was bombed in 1941, and it seemed that the new young Elizabeth II was to be denied the sacred anointing oil of her predecessors.

An elderly member of the Household remembered that King George VI had kept a tiny bottle as a valued memento but a thorough search at Buckingham Palace and Windsor Castle revealed no trace of the relic. The King's chemists seemed an obvious lead, but the firm that had made up the original prescription for Queen Victoria had gone out of business. The pharmacists who had compounded the anointing oil for George VI were then traced, one as far as Toronto, but both had died during the reign. The successors to their firm, however, still had the formula handed down since Charles II "Of pure myrrh one ounce, of sweet cinnamon half so much . . ." and so on, blending orange flowers, roses, musk, jasmine, flowers of benzoin, civet, ambergris and sweet calamus, among the forty ingredients. But modern chemists still could not be sure of the basic oil.

The investigators then decided to trace every family connection of Squire and Sons, the former royal chemists. Someone remembered a director who had boasted about the interesting souvenirs he had at home, and especially of a phial of pale golden oil once displayed in the window of a chemist's shop as an attraction. The trail led to a country house on the outskirts of Lingfield in Surrey, and to a white-haired lady who agreed quietly, "You have come to the right place."

The family had four ounces of the original base, still unrancid although it had been blended for the Coronation of Queen Victoria. Consecrated anew, two ounces were used for the anointing oil of Queen Elizabeth—and two ounces are still preserved for the future.

The Coronation planners breathed anew as if they had overcome a crucial hazard, and among them were none unsentimental enough to ask what it mattered.

Since Biblical times, the anointing of kings and queens has been a sacrament second only to the crowning. In the Regalia itself the Ampulla or gold vessel to contain the oil is of twelfth-century workmanship and may thus link Elizabeth II with the coronation of Henry IV back in 1399, before even Martin Luther, Christopher Columbus or Shakespeare were born. Such pledges of the past perhaps explain the zest in 1953 with which the British peoples devoted themselves to an affirmation of the continuity and tradition in which they excel.

Six months of intensive planning led into the final six months' taskwork of construction. A passionate desire for perfection in every detail of the Coronation became a national and indeed a Commonwealth obsession and, as the details gradually unfolded, the Queen herself became a foremost enthusiast in the quest for the ideal.

Six successive monarchs, for instance, had been content to use the ancient Coronation Chair in Westminster Abbey without over-close scrutiny of its parts.

The Queen however authorised that the layers of rude and ugly varnish should be stripped away. Beneath it the experts discovered traces of the rich gilding and colour painted at the time of Edward I, including the glass enamel with which the Chair was once jewelled. And so the Queen received her crowning not on a rotting worm-infested chair but on a traditional throne restored to finer state than it had seen for centuries.

Esconced beneath it, too, the famous Stone of Destiny was safe. After its theft by Scottish Nationalists and its due return in 1950, eccentric threats were made that the Stone would again disappear and perhaps be irretrievably shattered by explosives, threats which Scotland Yard took so seriously that the stone was concealed beneath a heavy flagstone in the Abbey vaults, and detectives kept special watch the night before the Coronation while workmen removed the paving slab with block and tackle and hauled the Stone of Scone to its rightful place.

The Crown jewels were, of course, always recognised to be in peril, especially the Crown of State with its 2,783 diamonds, which had to leave the Tower of London at an early stage to be dismantled and altered to fit the Queen. This Crown, in fact, was taken from the Tower, packed in a hatbox, in an ordinary saloon car with nothing to indicate that the driver and passengers in fact constituted an armed military escort. The plain-clothes crew of the accompanying police car were, I am told, armed only with truncheons.

When the entire Regalia, including the St Edward's Crown used for the ceremony of coronation, was moved from the Tower, a more subtle ruse was employed. Orb and Sceptre, jewelled swords and insignia all in reality travelled in a lorry curtained by tarpaulin. At the same time, however, a replica set of the Crown Jewels, similarly packed in leather cases, travelled through the streets of

London with a more obvious police guard. Equally cleaned and refurbished, these were the past replicas used in rehearsals. But even rehearsals stopped short of the actual crowning of the Queen, and Her Majesty never in fact wore a crown until the Coronation ceremony itself.

At the coronation of George VI a piece of red thread was discreetly placed to distinguish the back of the Crown from the front. Even so, it remained so inconspicuous that the Archbishop thought the thread had been removed and the King was very nearly crowned the wrong way round.

To avoid this embarrassment, the Queen had two silver stars affixed to the velvet, clearly apparent to even the most short-sighted Prelate. Yet worse pitfalls lurked in the ceremonial.

Several pieces of the Regalia were to be carried on velvet cushions in the Abbey procession. The gold lace ornamentation of the cushions aroused anxious debate when a senior official recalled that in 1937 the lace nearly caused disaster.

The Marquess of Salisbury, while carrying St Edward's Crown on its cushion, had entangled his Garter insignia in the lace and had to tear the lace from its cushion to twist himself free. Processing behind him, the Duke of Portland, carrying the Queen Consort's crown, was in even worse plight. The pendent of his Garter collar became so firmly attached that the magnificent Garter King of Arms had to come to his rescue. As a result, scrolled gold lace was absent from the Regalia cushions in 1953.

Even the short upright pile of the Coronation carpet, silky and smooth, had to be woven to precise specifications. At an earlier coronation, when a heavy long-piled carpet was used, the long trains of the peers and peeresses brushed the pile one way coming in, and the other way going out, creating a resistance so exhausting that some of the ancient nobility had to go home by ambulance.

Nothing like this occurred when Templeton's wove the carpet for Elizabeth II, an extraordinary one-piece carpet seventeen feet wide and over sixty yards long. With another carpet over thirty feet wide, the total weight of five tons presented special difficulty in transport into the Abbey.

The only other five-tonner in sight was the gilded State Coach in which the Queen would ride to and from her Coronation . . . and here the planners made a curious discovery. No one had foreseen that the Queen would come to the Throne when still so young and, until her accession, only one man had taken any decisive action towards the details of her Coronation. This was the Queen's own father, King George VI.

In 1951 he had caused the State Coach to be closely examined, and his experts had disturbing news. The fine old vehicle—completed in 1762 for King George III—was in a shocking state. Its chief glory, the seven panels painted by G.B. Cipriani, were cracked and brittle with age. The interior had not been re-upholstered since the Coronation of Queen Victoria and the great wheels were twisted and out of true. King George VI had however ordered the task of restoration to begin and the work was thus well advanced when his daughter came to the throne. The old wheels could not be brought back to true, but were successfully fitted with rubber tyres to lessen discomfort to passengers.

Meanwhile, the press of half the world took up a hot pursuit of the State Coach's coachman. What would it be like to drive the Queen on the great day, the cynosure of all eyes? An American magazine cabled its London editor to get the story at all costs. But Commander Colville, the Queen's Press Secretary, blandly explained that the State Coach has no coachman.

The coachman's box seat had been dismantled on the orders of Edward VII over sixty years ago, and the State Coach is drawn by mounted postillions. This disappointment did not deter the photographers who posed another Royal Mews Coachman in his gold and rose-feathered tricorne hat and gold-trimmed tunic alongside the State Coach. The resulting picture, though wildly inaccurate, was a world-wide success.

In fact, behind the scenes, George Hopkins, the Superintendent of the Royal Mews, faced a serious shortage of both coaches and coachmen. The Queen ardently wished to have a horsed Coronation procession to and from the Abbey. When her father came to the Throne, the Royal Mews had been crowded with coaches and carriages of every size. Unluckily, in a mood of stringent economy, shortly after the war, more than half were sold.

Some had been bought by Sir Alexander Korda for use on film sets—and he fortunately agreed to lend five two-pair broughams and two open landaus for a glittering farewell appearance in the royal pageantry of real life. Perhaps he realized that the loan gave the fleet of carriages enhanced value, for they were subsequently advertised for sale in a Hollywood trade journal, "recently reconditioned . . . as borrowed by the Crown for the Coronation".

The scarcity of coachmen presented a different dilemma. By long custom Her Majesty's coachmen and postillions are clean-shaven, and although ten members of the Coaching Club volunteered to serve the Queen they all sported magnificent moustaches. They needed no second bidding to make the ultimate sacrifice, and they shaved off their whiskers.

Moreover, all the Queen's horses were insufficient for the great procession. Some were borrowed from the Army, others from the brewers who were proud to employ the last dray-horses in London.

In the intricate mesh of detail, the grand plan of the Coronation moved to its culmination and surprisingly little was overlooked. Even the 430 wands to be carried by Coronation ushers received due attention. They were traditionally supposed to be of beech and the Duke of Norfolk sent a load of seasoned beechwood to the Crown Jewellers from his Arundel estate.

All the Queen's men, in fact, toiled for perfection but in the end, it must be said, they overlooked the greatest feminine need of a young and beautiful Queen on the most momentous day of her life.

Happily, the Queen's dresser, Miss Margaret MacDonald, the indefatigable Bobo, left nothing to chance and she paid a visit to Westminster Abbey three days beforehand to inspect the robing-rooms in the newly-built Annexe. The gilded furnishings, the tapestries and rich carpets were all in place. Everything had been done for the Queen's private comfort amid the pomp and splendour . . . except that no one had thought to provide the Queen and her ladies with mirrors.

Sander Zarach, a London mirror manufacturer, received the order to make and fit the mirrors only two days before the Coronation. His staff worked non-stop for thirty-six hours to make sixteen mirrors to the special specifications. The last looking-glass was installed only a few hours before the Queen arrived.

In the hectic hard-hammering final weeks before the Coronation, an extraordinary change meanwhile came over the heart of London. Staid old buildings were engulfed in wooden grandstands. The stands in turn became embowered in flowers and bunting. Altogether, public seating was devised for 110,000 people, in addition to the seats of 7,000 in an equally transfigured Abbey. A canvas city of tents also covered the green acres of Kensington Gardens to accommodate the troops who would line the streets or march in the procession.

No fewer than 43,000 soldiers came from overseas, and the Orders for Troops covered every contingency. "Fainting is very catching. Platoon commanders must keep constant watch.... Anyone showing distress will be ordered to ground arms and step to the rear. His head will be held down between his knees by the man next to him."

In the Abbey, too, the Queen's Maids of Honour were to conceal easily crushable phials of smelling salts within their white gloves, a precaution that later saved at least one of the six ladies, who suddenly found the strong TV lights too oppressive.

As the months of complex co-ordination sped towards fulfilment, a Minister of the Crown visited the toilets in Hyde Park to decide whether these indispensable hutments should be painted in conspicuous red and grey stripes or more delicate grey and primrose. In the Abbey, retiring rooms were marked "Ladies" and "Peeresses", but there were finer points of precedence. Peers and peeresses of lesser grades had to ballot for Abbey seats, so tight was space. The disappointed were comforted by seats in the street stands with the added amenity of extra seats for guests available at £6 a head. Informed of his Abbey reservation, the Paramount Chief of Barotseland was told that Regulations would not preclude his carrying a ceremonial horsehair fly whisk. Seventy Gold Coast Chiefs, on the other hand, rejected stand seats outside the Abbey which they considered beneath their dignity. Few Londoners would have objected to such humilation, and one man turned up at the Abbey with a forged invitation, the victim of a young Hull apprentice printer who prepared and sent out a score of hoax invitations, which the police thought would not deceive a child. The police had prepared elaborate measures against gatecrashers, but this hoodwinked unfortunate turned out to be the only one.

London crowds are noted for their orderly good humour. Yet in actual fact Coronation Day produced 6,873 casualties, ten per cent of them serious ambulance cases. Legs were broken under crowd pressure. In their determination to miss nothing, some people suffered from exposure after spending the night on wet pavements. Child casualties were unexpectedly few. Military casualties, however, included many soldiers who were nicked by bayonets, while troops were turning the street corners in smart formation.

And certainly the crowds were the largest the metropolis had ever seen. Eager, curious, excited, joyful, they ultimately focussed in police statistics one single clue of extraordinary loyalty. Even the crooks were on their best behaviour. A police commissioner was able to report the astonishing fact that, despite their presence in any large crowd, pickpockets were *entirely inactive* on Coronation Day.

For the personal preparations of the Queen herself, the ballroom and art gallery at Buckingham Palace were marked out with measured white tapes to conform to the size of the Coronation theatre in Westminster Abbey, and ordinary chairs served as thrones and faldstools. The first Abbey rehearsal was held on 14 May, when the clergy practised their procession and duties and the musicians and choir were present. Next day the Duchess of Norfolk deputized for the Queen in a full enactment of the ceremony with the Archbishop of Canterbury. The Queen first visited the Abbey and watched rehearsals ten days before the real ceremony. The mock Regalia now glittered on the high altar. The Duchess of Norfolk, with a train pinned to her everyday dress, advanced in a procession down the nave . . .

The Queen knew her role so well that her attendance at another rehearsal was deemed unnecessary. Nor was she ever crowned "in replica". The Duchess of Norfolk wore the replica again and again and, at the final great dress rehearsal, when the Queen was not present, her husband congratulated her on "a superb performance".

After so much preparation and painstaking care for the meshwork of ceremonial, Coronation Day itself dawned with the weather dull and despirited. For the Queen, awakened by the murmur of the crowds, it must have reminded her vividly of her father's Coronation Day, during her childhood, when she confided to her journal, "At five o'clock in the morning I was woken up by the band of the Royal Marines striking up just outside my window. I lept out of bed. . . . We put on dressing-gowns and shoes and Bobo made me put on an eiderdown as it was so cold and we crouched in the window looking on to a cold misty morning. There were already some people in the stands and all the time people were coming to them in a stream . . ."

In 1953 the first ushers were in the Abbey at 6 a.m. Within the next hour the troops began marching into position to line the route. At 8.45 the Lord Mayor arrived in his coach at Westminster Abbey, and at that hour a score of cleaners were still brushing the carpet.

The television team, 120 strong, had been at their posts at 7 a.m. The broadcast was due to start at 10.15 a.m., with a live "hook-up" to 200 relaying stations in Europe and, at five minutes to ten, a complete sound failure occurred at the one essential TV switching point in Broadcasting House. Tense minutes ensued until technicians located and replaced the faulty power cable and all was well. There was, however, another last-minute hitch in which the Queen was more vitally concerned.

Twenty minutes before Her Majesty was due to enter the State Coach it was discovered that two large buckles containing the trace which linked all eight horses had after cleaning and overhaul been sewn on back to front, a serious weakness factor which might cause the buckles to give way.

Without marring the split-second programme there was no time to remove and reverse the buckles until the Queen was safely at the Abbey. The superintendent in charge of the procession, superintendent Hopkins had to take a chance. And so the Queen stepped into her Coach unaware of anything wrong . . . and save for the tropic downpours of rain nothing else went amiss that day.

The Duke of Norfolk as Earl Marshal had announced three

months beforehand that the Queen would be crowned "at about 12.34". The crowning in fact occurred at 12.33 and 30 seconds. When the Crown was settled on her head, the Queen momentarily steadied it with her hand. When Prince Philip knelt in fealty, swearing to become her liege man, he then kissed her on the left cheek, accidentally touching the Crown so that it slipped slightly and the Queen adjusted it again.

Presently, wearing her Crown Of State, carrying her Orb and Sceptre, the slender young woman and her husband went out to the gold coach, to the ringing bells and the cheers, mile upon mile, the enthusiasm of the crowds unquenched although the London rain lashed down on the multitude.

What was the Queen's own impression? That evening she broadcasted to her peoples and said, quietly and gently, "As this day draws to its close I know that my abiding memory will be, not only the solemnity and beauty of the ceremony, but the inspiration of your loyalty and affection." The draft text was written in advance but the two last words, I understand, were added impromptu by the Queen herself.

10 The Queen's Treasures

A close look at the accessories and comforts of royal glamour.

Her Majesty, Connoisseur

When the Queen was a child and first heard that she was going to live in Buckingham Palace with her parents, she said in reluctant tones, "You mean *for ever*?"

To the young Princess the treasure-filled rooms of the vast Palace seemed like a museum, as any fine collection of antique furniture and *objets d'art* may do to the uninstructed eye.

Then her grandmother, Queen Mary, began taking her on little tours of the State Apartments, telling her the special story of each priceless piece in her fabulous heritage. Today, when the Queen herself is chatelaine of the royal palaces, connoisseurs are continually surprised at her wide knowledge.

When King Baudouin of the Belgians and Queen Fabiola stayed at the Palace, their hostess praised the refinements of Belgian craftsmanship and took pride in displaying some of her finest pieces of French furniture. Unlike many experts, the Queen knew that the supreme eighteenth century cabinet-makers practised their skills in Belgium before emigrating to Paris.

Guests often admire the exquisite marquetry of a mahogany and tulipwood bureau usually to be seen in the White Drawing Room, and said to be by Riesener, one of the best-known of all French furniture designers. The Queen was delighted when modern scientific scrutiny recently disclosed a monogram proving its authenticity beyond dispute.

In her other White Drawing Room, at Windsor Castle, the Queen has a jewel cabinet of superb beauty by the same master.

After the French Revolution, republicans auctioned the furnishings; and British secret agents eagerly snapped up many items for King George IV. Yet probably few people realize that many of the fine pieces that graced Versailles and the Petit-Luxembourg are now owned by the Queen and, like every connoisseur, she enjoys a story of a good bargain. That great piece was purchased at auction by George IV for only £420. Another of her special treasures is a richly ornamented chest of drawers with two corner cupboards en suite which stood in Louis XVI's private study. A rash assessor once valued the chest alone at £50,000, but the three together are probably priceless and they cost only £107. 2s. at the Paris auction. No doubt the extra bid of two shillings—a few francs—closed the deal.

All the royal furniture seems flawless, as you realize when cherished pieces are displayed in the Queen's Gallery from time to time. Yet the Queen likes to tell of a writing table of unrivalled William and Mary style which was almost unrecognisable under the dust of a Windsor photographic studio some years ago. The marquetry veneering had risen in the damp and partly disappeared. The woodworm was so bad that the weight of the top could scarcely be borne on the tottering legs. The task of expert repair took five months' incessant work and was well worth-while. Documentary evidence came to light that the writing table was the one used by King William himself, and the piece—the quintessence of a period—was restored to its original beauty.

Indeed, I have just been privileged to browse through the "housekeeping catalogue" used by the Queen's grandmother, Queen Mary, when she was so busy rescuing many old and precious furnishings from neglect. It is full of fascinating notes about the finds made in Castle cellars and attics.

In a "mysterious black hole", for instance, was found a charming pine medicine cabinet, with all its ebony pharmacy jars and velvet-lined herbal drawers, a complete apothecary's store. Moreover, it was of the finest German work of about the year 1685 and was standing on a later table made by Chippendale himself. It turned out to be the medicine chest of King Charles II.

Two superb silver tables of the seventeenth century have also long been among the Queen's choicest possessions. But Queen

Mary's catalogue tells how three matching silver mirrors were retrieved from a lumber-room where they had been stored for over 100 years. The Queen's red ribbon bookmark, too, marks an exciting clue in a treasure hunt. The notes tell of a *third* silver table which got broken and was put into store. By degrees its silver bullion was despoiled for its intrinsic value, and the carcass of the vanished table has never been found.

The bulk of the Queen's wonderful furniture has, of course, been carefully tended for generations. Even Queen Charlotte's delightful sedan-chair, all gilt and crimson, has been handed down through successive members of the Royal Family and still has its original glass in the windows. If you are interested in unusual mementos, Windsor Castle shelters a surpassing oddity in the armchair carved by Chippendale's son from an elm-tree that stood in the centre of the British army lines at the Battle of Waterloo. And in the Blue Drawing Room at Buckingham Palace is a comparatively small occasional table that belonged to Napoleon, its top of Sèvres porcelain adorned with the medallion heads of twelve commanders of antiquity.

King George IV prized this relic so highly that he had it included as an accessory in several of his official portraits. Thanks to this monarch's lavish expenditure for Carlton House, and Brighton Pavilion and elsewhere, our queen's homes are well stocked with choice specimens of Hepplewhite, Sheraton and other English designers. In the Palace Throne Room moreover are two armchairs of carved and gilded wood, with backs fashioned like Roman chariots, which some authorities suggest are the finest examples of Regency furniture ever made.

Despite the Queen's deep pride in her rich family heirlooms, it must be said however that her best-loved and most-used furnishings are of a simpler kind. In the main, they are the wedding gifts with which she first created her home as a bride, and these sentimental treasures still effectively set the key in her private rooms.

The cascade of light in a cut-glass chandelier, the deep tones of polished wood, the flawless embroidery of an old firescreen are elements from which the Queen derives a satisfying feminine pleasure.

Family sentiment is implicit in a Hepplewhite mahogany break-front bookcase, bought for her by the joint subscription of many of her closest relatives. Behind the lozenge-shaped glazing, the Queen keeps not books but some of the lovely smaller gifts presented to her on State Occasions. Below the shelves on which these are displayed, an array of drawers and cupboards also contribute a solution to personal storage problems. For many years the Queen has had a chest-of-drawers in her living-room—an elegant satinwood chest, circa 1780, serpentine-fronted—and everything from children's toys, a table-cloth or a pile of magazines can be conveniently popped into it.

Then there is "Granny's screen", a fourfold screen mounted with needlework which was a wedding gift from Queen Mary. In the first sitting-room that she planned as a bride, the then Princess Elizabeth based her colour scheme on its coral, Chinese yellow and turquoise blue. Today I believe it still gives useful service to conceal the unavoidable clutter of a writing table when required. Some people no doubt imagine it is an oriental prize from perhaps Peking or Canton. In reality, it was made in Cambridge.

One of the Queen's family gifts also comprise a drawing-room suite of eight armchairs and two settees painted and gilt in the Louis XV taste. A French diplomat once admired it enthusiastically, perhaps finding that it appealed to his national pride. But the original bill had accompanied the gift as part of its pedigree, and the Queen refrained from mentioning that the suite had been made by an eighteenth century English cabinet-maker in a workshop in Berkeley Square.

No survey of the Queen's treasures can ever be complete. When Her Majesty restored some of the exotic Chinese and Indian furnishings to Brighton Pavilion their places were filled by plainer pieces—chests of blonde mahogany with simple rather than ornate inlays of satinwood, classical sofa-tables in warm thuya wood. The Queen has a pair of occasional chairs in painted imitation of bamboo, and these two fragile yet restful pieces hold their own in the Palace atmosphere.

The Queen's Wonderful Silver

Within the domestic environs of Buckingham Palace is a range of seven kitchen rooms and strongrooms, romantically known by old custom as the Silver Pantry. With its walls lined by cupboards massed with velvet-hooded pieces, its racks piled with mysterious chests and leather cases, this secret domain has the air of a workshop rather than an Aladdin's Cave. Yet if all the Queen's silver could be placed on display, the baize-aproned polishers know that it would dazzle the world. I was recently privileged to look through the inventories of this unrivalled collection and the three great volumes, crested with the Royal Arms and bound in tooled red morocco leather, hold a special enchantment.

How many silver spoons, knives and forks, do you suppose, has the Queen? In fiddle-and-shell pattern alone, the royal store includes eighteen *dozen* teaspoons, eighteen dozen breakfast knives, four dozen egg-spoons . . . and thirty egg-cups to match.

Despite meticulous housekeeping, spoons occasionally disappear in every home. In the royal household accidental losses are made good from time to time by sending old unwanted plate to be melted down and moulded anew into standard patterns in use.

An unmanageably heavy silver teapot—given by the King of Madagascar to Queen Victoria—was serviceably recast in this way, and four dozen teaspoons to replenish one set were created from the silver of fifty-one huge and rather ugly Chinese coins which Oriental scholars agreed were neither of antiquarian interest nor modern value.

Although a little silver night-light perhaps had some charm, even that inflexible curator, Queen Mary, approved its transformation into tableware, and a gigantic Victorian silver cup must have been a nightmare to polish until its 210 ounces went to the melting pot. All these conversions are carefully noted in the royal ledgers, so that the fate of a silver "white elephant" can always be traced.

Everyone has heard of the Queen's magnificent gold plate, ranging as it does from a fabulous twelve-branched 2,722-ounce candelabra to the wonderful artistry of the centrepieces fashioned by Paul

Storr, the gifted goldsmith of Regency days. One should perhaps explain that the gold plate is actually silver gilt, made of solid silver plated with gold, for solid gold itself is too soft and lacks sparkle.

In practical terms, there are twenty-four dozen gold table plates matched by only 8 dozen soup plates, but plates in another pattern are used when necessary to make up. For State banquets, over 100 gold salt-cellars can complement this array.

Some say that the largest dish displayed on the sideboard on State occasions, the so-called Shield of Achilles, thirty-seven inches in diameter, looks just a little like a Turkish brass coffee tray. Yet every State piece has individual splendour. One can picture the lavish atmosphere of an Edwardian court ball at which a single silver punch-bowl could dispense over 200 glassfuls to the guests!

In piquant contrast, only four simple silver salt-cellars are catalogued for the royal nursery at Windsor and there are only two nursery sugar-tongs. Not long ago Prince Andrew and Prince Edward held a party for fifty of their young friends and the everyday silver was reinforced by two dozen nursery teaspoons dating back to 1854.

The pencilled notes in the silver inventories, indeed, are fascinating. One can imagine the blushes when a 200-year-old cruet from the Steward's Room was found to be broken not long ago. There are souvenir hunters even at Buckingham Palace, and silver cork mounts are particularly liable to disappear. One one occasion, a stocktaking disclosed that no fewer than thirteen silver-mounted carving knives were missing, a Palace Pantry mystery that has never been solved.

Happily, there are finds to be chronicled as well as losses. Queen Mary dearly loved a sugar castor that had once belonged to Queen Anne and was overjoyed when she found its twin in the saleroom. Both are still in use at our own Queen's table today. Like her grandmother, the Queen also occasionally attends an auction private view and is delighted when some missing piece of historic or sentimental interest can be purchased and restored to the royal collection.

In the old days so much table silver was melted down or sold with each successive new reign that little early date remains. In the

State Apartments at Windsor you may see a pair of silver-mounted bellows once used by Nell Gwynn and, apart from altar plate, this is one of the few pieces dating to Charles II.

An ink-stand and a wine cooler of great splendour are among the few treasures handed down from Queen Anne. King George III was content to buy little silver save for two or three French tureens which were purchased second-hand in the post-Revolution era. His son, George IV, was the gold-and-silversmiths' first lavish royal patron.

For this very reason the Queen has taken an evident pride in building up her own personal collection of early English and Scottish domestic silver. It began with her wedding gifts, when one friend gave her a set of six apostle spoons with early Exeter marks of the seventeenth century and another group of friends subscribed to purchase a set of graceful silver candlesticks of the year 1771.

The Queen Mother also bought for her daughter a silver tea-tray, unusual in that it bears the arms of George III and thus must have been a gift of the King to a foreign ambassador, a reminder to the Queen of the subtle role that a monarch can play in diplomacy. Her Majesty also has a pair of silver cups displaying the art that the Huguenot refugees brought as silversmiths to this country.

As distinct from the rich Crown collection, the Queen's personal silver is mostly of the simple kind that you might find at any tea-table. Coffee-pots are still made in the style of Queen Anne, with scrolled wooden handles, and the Queen possesses an authentic coffee-pot of the year 1713. Overseas visitors frequently come to Britain hoping to buy old silver, but one would be fortunate indeed to discover such a treasure as a cake-basket dated 1756, fashioned in delicate silver trelliswork, which the Queen owns.

Connoisseurs know that complete tea-services were not introduced until about 1730 but the Queen often uses a Scottish service with a teapot known to have been made in 1715. It bears the rarest of Aberdeen hallmarks, although the square tray, sugar bowl and cream jug, were not made until fifteen years afterwards. The teapot of another of the Queen's prized Scottish services has an Edinburgh hallmark of 1726. Here again the other pieces do not quite match and were not, in fact, made until a score of years later.

Once, when I was helping a bride to buy one or two items of old silver, she refused to consider pieces bearing the initials of earlier owners. Yet one cannot of course buy *new* old silver, and it is of interest that many of the pieces in the Queen's personal collection bear the inscriptions of other families. A lovely silver-gilt epergne—a table centre-piece—is not less beautiful because it bears the arms of the first Lord Lonsdale. A cake-basket is all the more treasured for her Sandringham tea-table because its inscription reveals earlier links with Norfolk.

Should one inscribe old silver nowadays? For most of us the answer surely is that except for day-to-day rare antique pieces should be left in their natural time-worn state. A contemporary inscription, however, obviously meets with royal approval; and I notice that many of the Queen's treasures—trays and tea-caddies, sweetmeat baskets, entree dishes, salvers and salt-cellars—have been engraved with her bridal arms as Duchess of Edinburgh. Even the members of the Royal Academy considered an engraved inscription in order when they presented the Queen and her husband with a handsome silver dish made by the eighteenth century silversmith, Thomas Heming.

The Queen's silver demonstrates, moreover, that silver plate may equally merit admiration for its intrinsic beauty. The Queen's plated articles include candlesticks and kettles, knife-trays, nut crackers and much else. Many pieces in the family hoard of Victorian silver, once considered ugly and obsolete, have also by the circle of time passed into a phase of admiration. Prince Philip sent two opulent Victorian tea-kettles to the Royal College of Art not long ago and suggested that they should be converted with small electric immersion heaters. His ideas were skilfully carried out.

Above all, Queen Elizabeth II gives great encouragement to the modern silversmith. Made for her Coronation, a sumptuous vase, topped by a crown and bearing the arms of Commonwealth countries, past and present, evokes admiration at the dinners of Commonwealth Prime Ministers at the Palace. The Queen accords her patronage every year to a competition among craftsmen for the silver racing cups at Royal Ascot. The royal yacht *Britannia* similarly has its own silver, and a superb set of five pieces of

Communion plate in contemporary style was presented to the vessel not long ago.

Nowadays the Queen permits only drab and thoroughly worn-out plate to undergo conversion. Not long ago, the problem of finding a new use for twenty-four ormolu miniature coats of arms puzzled everybody. Now they can be seen embellishing the hearth fenders throughout the State Apartments in Buckingham Palace!

The Queen's Crystal

When the Queen was still a young bride of not six months standing, her parents celebrated their own silver wedding . . . and the present Queen Mother gave her husband, King George VI, perhaps the most charming piece of engraved modern crystal ever fashioned. It was a casket in the form of a crystal temple that glittered in token of true love.

Today it is certain that both the Queen and her mother deeply cherish this family treasure as a unique and tender symbol of affection. The walls are glass panels engraved with symbols of her father's interests: with books, humble gardening tools, sporting trophies and the instruments of architecture and design. Upon the lid is inscribed a poem *From The Queen to The King*:

> "Fond hope: to compass on a page so brief
> The testament of Love!—on timid glass . . ."

The delightful idea of a temple has been maintained in every detail. One's admiring finger may gently mount four steps of macassar ebony around the base and push against a polished door. As this opens, light floods as if by magic through the translucent floor, and engravings of garlands and of Cupid's altar spring into shining relief. Swing the door again and the light fades. This is surely a treasure for all and yet the crystal casket is seldom seen by strangers, so intimate and personal is its theme.

The Queen's collection of crystal is inevitably overshadowed though not outshone by the fame of more substantial royal treasures. But the fragility of glass can be denied when one realizes that, in this field also, the Queen possesses services of toilet and table-ware dating back to Charles II and intricate specimens of Venetian glass of at least 100 years earlier.

At Sandringham is a case of glittering Chinese crystals modelled in exquisite flowers and figures and the Queen takes pleasure in rearranging and adding to this display from time to time. Another family collection of scent bottles of rock crystal and glass includes bibelots that once graced Queen Charlotte's dressing-table. At the same time, the Queen takes a personal delight in art of the modern glass engraver, as guests discover aboard the royal yacht *Britannia* where, in an ante-room of the royal apartments, an illuminated cabinet sets off a set of seven gold-rimmed glasses, each stippled to depict a home of the Queen. The picture on the central goblet shows the royal yacht itself. To each side are grouped slightly smaller glasses with air-twist stems, showing Windsor Castle, Balmoral, Sandringham, Buckingham Palace, Clarence House and even the Queen's childhood home at 145 Piccadilly.

This is so much to the Queen's liking that she and her husband once gave General de Gaulle a rather similar set of three, one inscribed, one engraved with a view of Windsor Castle as if caught in the rays of the evening sun, and the third with a view of Versailles glimmering in moonlight.

As with the *Britannia* set, and the ornament of King George's casket, the engraving was the work of Mr Laurence Whistler, surely the most accomplished of modern craftsmen. Yet he confesses that when he first "began to scratch glass" he knew nothing of the art or its history. He practised on windowpanes, like the Elizabethan courtiers, and then progressed to working on blown glass in the shape of old bottles and decanters. Ultimately he was commissioned to engrave a Georgian goblet as a wedding-gift to the Queen from one of her friends.

One remembers that President Truman of the United States also gave the Queen a lidded crystal bowl at that time, elaborately engraved with the youthful and fanciful theme of a merry-go-round. This gift was however equalled in magnificence by the great covered cup in crystal, The Queen's Cup, presented by President Eisenhower when the Queen and her husband visited America in

1957, in which every flower, bird and tree characteristic of the English-founded state of Virginia is seen in the design. Both these pieces are in Steuben glass, the finest America can provide, and both are engraved by Bruce Moore, enabling us to perceive the contrast of ten years in an artist-sculptor's development.

Once, when the former Mrs Jacqueline Kennedy (now Mrs Onassis) visited England and dined at the Palace, the Queen paid her guest a subtle compliment by using a table-setting of American crystal plates. Each of the twelve plates was engraved to represent a different bird from the old Audubon prints: a table service for preliminary beauty and elegance, of course, rather than everyday use. With these the Queen also has a set of candlesticks, a centre bowl and matching compotes of modern Steuben crystal, a gift from Mr and Mrs Harriman.

The royal crystal in most frequent use is probably a set of cut crystal heart-shaped salt spoons. Practical, beautiful, with a touch of novelty, these perfectly evoke the Queen's taste. The glassware on the royal table, too, has a quiet functional elegance. Made of Royal Brierley crystal of superb quality, the wine-glasses are plain but for the Royal Cipher, short-stemmed, broad-based and not readily upset. Deeper elaboration of cut is reserved for the decanters and butter dishes in the same pattern.

Characteristically, the Queen once visited Brierley Hill in Staffordshire to see how her table crystal was made. Technical information about the heavier lead oxides that distinguish crystal and glass perhaps left Her Majesty unmoved. But at a factory workbench she saw an elderly woman veteran cleaning the inside of a wine decanter and immediately asked, "I've often wondered how these are cleaned. Would you please show me?"

In the Glass Pantry at Buckingham Palace, soap and cold water and a nail-brush is effective for engraved glass, with a gadget like a long toothbrush for those difficult interior crannies.

There is a story of a connoisseur who was privileged to visit Buckingham Palace while compiling a handbook on crystal and glass. They took him first to the top of the Grand Staircase where the light pours through a dome of eighty glass panels each engraved with classical goddesses. He was then taken to see the two immense chandeliers in the Music Room, rising tier on tier in ormolu circles, which are considered the finest ever created. In another room he was shown that the facets of the chandeliers match those of the door-handles, the work of a Regency craftsman named Wainwright.

The handbook was never written, for the expert decided it would be impossible to describe these achievements in crystal and light that sparkle amid the mirrored doors and pier-glasses throughout the Palace. In her own private apartments, the Queen also has two chandeliers or lustres of Waterford glass, with icicle drops hung in festoons, which effectively deputize for sunlight on the darkest wintry day.

The Queen's favourite rose bowl was presented to her by the Worshipful Company of Glass Sellers and stands on a sapphire blue base, achieving a symphony of light and colour with its summer burden of flowers. At Balmoral, too, the Queen treasures a silver-mounted cut glass scent bottle, which originally contained perfume distilled from the flowers of royal Deeside and was a gift from the people of Crathie. And it is at Balmoral, again, that the Queen uses the set of Monart table glass in turquoise blue and gold which was a gift to her from the city of Perth.

Every piece of crystal around the Queen, indeed, sparkles with its own story. Her Faberge crystal inkstand was a precious wedding-gift—and even a crystal paperweight, sometimes seen in photographs of her desk, was a well-chosen presentation from a group of boy scouts.

Large and small, all these royal treasures glitter with true enchantment but, not least, I am tempted to mention a unique work in crystal owned by Queen Elizabeth the Queen Mother. Like her silver wedding casket, it was specially engraved by Laurence Whistler and it stands in daily use upon her desk, a crystal screen like a triple mirror.

The centre panel holds the typed sheet of her day's engagements. The right hand panel is inscribed with a verse upon her duties "*This tape to cut . . . that stone to lay . . .*" But the left-hand panel has a verse upon her pleasures, which I venture to quote more fully for the warm light it sheds upon a beloved royal lady:

PLEASURES—A myriad to rehearse!
The likely horse . . . the lucky "hand"
the leaping trout . . . The living verse
The favourite waltz . . . The floodlit dome
The crowds, the lights, the welcome . . . And
(Sweet as them all) the going home!

The Queen's Porcelain

Guests invited to royal garden parties at Buckingham Palace often approach the lawns through the Bow Room—and there invariably pause to admire the finest display of English porcelain in the world.

Arrayed in four handsome cabinets is a unique 200-years-old Chelsea dinner service. Magnificently decorated with gilded butterflies on "mazarin" blue and painted birds and flowers, it was originally a gift from King George III to his brother-in-law, the ruling Duke of Mecklenburg-Strelitz. People often imagine it to be among the oldest of family heirlooms. In reality, it remained in the ownership of the ducal family and then survived many adventures of the saleroom, including a perilous wartime crossing of the Atlantic—and was eventually presented to Queen Elizabeth the Queen Mother and made over by Her Majesty in turn to the Crown collection.

Nearby in the Bow Room are two clocks in cases of Chelsea porcelain, replete with exquisite figures of shepherds and their maids, modelled in the few brief years when the Chelsea factory produced its masterpieces. The Queen herself characteristically arranged that these treasures should be placed where they meet as many appreciative eyes as possible. And at the entrance of the State Apartments in Windsor Castle, as I write, new lighting is to embellish the dozen richly filled showcases, on view to the public, that might well be termed the royal china museum.

Hurried visitors may accord the varied pieces and sets a casual glance while the knowledgeable linger in fuller enjoyment. Here is a precious set of dark blue Royal Worcester, made for the Prince Regent in the year of Waterloo. There is royal blue Minton made a century ago for Queen Victoria and another Minton set decorated in sublty different royal blue for King Edward VII.

When her Italian art treasures were put on show in the Queen's Gallery, the Queen similarly decided to display her "Etruscan Service" of Italian porcelain as a dazzling centrepiece. Once a gift from the King of Naples to George III, painted in red enamel, with designs inspired or adapted from antique models, the examples of this fabulous 282-piece service provided an ideal foil to the pictures and sculpture.

Again, the Queen possesses one of the finest collections of Sèvres in the world . . . sumptuous pot-pourri vases that enhance the furniture of the State rooms, tureens of turquoise blue that are often filled with flowers, jardinières that actually date from 1753, the year the Sèvres factory was founded. A splendid Sèvres dessert service decorates a glazed cupboard in the Household dining-room at Buckingham Palace as if to make every official aware of the constant pressure of royal storage problems.

Amid these ancestral heirlooms, the Queen naturally has a feminine preference for her "very own" Sèvres. A delightful tea service of 1768 in blue and gold was a wedding gift from the Rothschilds; and on special occasions the Queen uses a modern Sèvres dinner service bearing her own personal cipher, bordered in mist blue and gold tracery, a gift from the people of France.

The Queen Mother trained both her daughters in the appreciation of fine china, and the Queen was encouraged to form her own collection of pottery figures—dogs and horses, dainty fawns and similar subjects—when she was still a young girl. Princess Anne has formed a similar small collection. In a glass-fronted Hepplewhite case in the Queen's private apartments are other separate pieces, each with a pleasant personal association. One might mention a charming Dresden pair of playful Cupids, for example, a highly appropriate presentation from an infant welfare centre. A blue Delft plate of the seventeenth century, painted with a lively Flemish scene, was a gift from the British women of The Hague. An old Spode jug strikes a homely note with its posy of wax flowers. Sculptured among delicate porcelain daffodils, a superbly modelled American robin recalls a visit to the United States and the vigorous figure of a polo player was a gift from President and Mrs Eisenhower.

Fragile china is as liable to get smashed in a royal household as anywhere else. When a wedding-gift vase underwent a mishap, the Queen had it repaired so perfectly that the donor could not tell the difference. A group of antique dealers once offered the Queen the remnants of a William IV dessert service although, under the buffets of time, only twelve plates remained. But the Queen was delighted to have them for sentiment's sake.

Provided no irreparable harm is done to the porcelain, it is clear that the Queen agrees with those who deem the beauty of an old vase enhanced with a shade for use as a table lamp. Her aunt, Lady Rose Granville, once gave her a Chinese vase arranged as a lamp, embossed with figures in famille rose enamels that seem to glow in the light. The Queen's great friends, Lord and Lady Rupert Nevill, once equally struck her taste with a table lamp of Chinese white porcelain engraved with patterns of flowers, used for many years close to her favourite armchair. In another room, two Coalbrookdale vases also form table lamps and, here again, the soft downward glow dramatises the theme of Scottish eagles modelled in high relief amid flowers and foliage. And here one may add a charming idea hitherto known to only the Queen's closer friends. Her Majesty has a pair of bedside lamps in flowered Stoke china—and a breakfast service for two to match.

In royal residences so well-stocked with family treasures, it remains evident that the Queen has created an atmosphere of her own. The change may lie in refinements that pass almost unnoticed. On one of the chimneypieces of Buckingham Palace there once stood a cumbersome French clock which seemed to sprout oddly from two Chinese figures in Vincennes porcelain.

The Queen saw that the clock had nothing to do with this charmingly modelled little group, a playful Oriental boy and girl, and it had in fact been added some sixty years ago. Now the clock has been detached and banished, and the mantelpiece could have no finer adornment than the mischievous Chinese boy and his amusing almond-eyed companion.

Elsewhere, throughout Buckingham Palace, so many superlative pieces in the Chinese taste are in evidence that it is difficult to single out this or that favourite for public attention. On a console table in the Yellow Drawing-Room, for instance, one is tempted to admire the freshness of three groups of flowers apparently planted in boxes of old Japanese lacquer. One has to look closer to discover that the flowers are artificial ... with a difference. Narcissus, daffodils, tulips, pinks, anemones, they originally blossomed for Louis XV and have flowered unharmed for 200 years as flawless examples of the finest Vincennes porcelain.

Inevitably, one may come to wonder which tableware the Queen prefers for her personal use. Among all the breakfast tables of Britain, only the Queen can commence her day with a breakfast set of Royal Worcester in royal blue and gold given to her by the City of Worcester. Another modern breakfast service of white chain decorated with green laurel leaves is also favoured.

When Count de Poiret, the equestrian artist, was the Queen's guest for a week at Windsor, he was delighted to find that a different dessert service was used every day, With the set of Royal Copenhagen painted with different flowers, the Coalport on a theme of fruit and foliage, the Old Rockingham and Spode, each with bouquets of flowers, the royal changes could have been rung for quite a while.

Amused at such an array, a guest once wondered aloud what might be used for a night cup of cocoa or chocolate. So the story goes, and the Queen is said to have shown him her wonderful set of twelve two-handled Dresden chocolate cups. Finished inside with finely burnished gold, dated 1780, this astonishing set—a personal gift from Pope Pius XII—ranks of course as one of the treasures of Windsor and is never used.

Yet the Queen regularly uses a dinner service that money could not buy, although the replacement of breakages is not too difficult. This is the dinner service of Royal Worcester specially made for her and presented to Her Majesty by the Brigade of Guards. Of palest ivory within a gold border, each piece bears the crest of one of the five regiments forming the Brigade. Simple, modern, richly beautiful and unique, it is indeed a dinner service fit for the Queen.

The Queen's Bibelots

It is remembered of the Queen, as a little girl, that she carefully saved her pennies to help buy a Christmas gift for her grandfather, King George V. All the Royal Family, indeed, subscribed to a very special Christmas present one year... and when the old King unwrapped the tiny gift package at Sandringham it truly proved to be a charming surprise.

For out popped an elephant—a perfect miniature not two inches long, with ivory tusks and ruby eyes. On its back, robed in white enamel, an Indian Mahout sat on a yellow gold rug patterned with rose diamonds. One of the stones could be moved aside and a gold key inserted to wind the mechanism. Then by pressing a tiny lever in the harness the elephant plodded forward, swinging head and tail. The old King was delighted, and jovially insisted on showing "my christmas elephant" to every visitor. Today it still enchants newcomers to Sandringham.

At Windsor an even smaller toy—Queen Mary's gold-mounted grand piano, 1½ inches high—links the spirit of Christmas past with present-day fun.

All the world knows of the wonderful royal Collection of paintings and furniture, but the Queen is also chatelaine of less familiar collections—of Queen Mary's richly adorned scent-bottles and gold boxes and jades, Queen Alexandra's Fabergé treasures and Queen Victoria's fans and cameos... all the entrancing small curios and objects of art that experts call the Queen's bibelots.

When this century was young, for instance, King Edward VII invariably solved his gift problem by giving his wife an exquisite new piece by the Russian court goldsmith and craftsman, Carl Fabergé. Queen Alexandra adored them. One Christmas she was presented with a ruby-eyed rabbit, carved in pure white chalcedony. Another time three of her favourite dogs were modelled in vari-coloured agate, watched by three tiny mice with rose diamond eyes.

Today the Queen has assembled the Fabergé figures in skilfully lit display cases at Sandringham to captivate children and connoisseurs

For his first art purchase Prince Philip directly commissioned Stella Marks to paint this charming miniature portrait of his bride.

(See PRINCE PHILIP'S PAINTINGS)

(ABOVE) *Prince Philip purchased these theatrical porcelain figures modelled by Brigette Appleby. From left to right: Vivien Leigh, Sir Laurence Olivier, Paul Robeson and Sir John Gielgud.*

(See PRINCE PHILIP'S PAINTINGS)

(BELOW) *Scottish art students admire a painting purchased by Prince Philip*

alike. Here is a diamond-eyed hornbill, its gold claws firmly perched in a 2½-inch silver-gilt cage. One cabinet shelf is devoted to the richest model farm ever assembled. A team of artists made wax models of favourite Sandringham animals and then these were sent to Russia for Fabergé to create his replicas in precious metals and jewels. The shire horse has eyes of cabochon sapphires. The ducklings waddle on red gold legs. The cockerel is made of obsidian, a rare volcanic stone.

There are miniature flowers set out for admiration in small glass containers. A spray of japonica rises from a tumbler of water but the blossoms are actually of enamelled gold and both the glass and the liquid in it are a superb illusion carved from a single piece of rock-crystal. In separate rock-crystal pots are enamelled rosebuds, carnations and sprays of catkin and wild cherry of unbelievable realism, their leaves carved in jade.

Queen Mary loved these treasures and collected many of her own, including miniature French furniture with tabletops of mother-of-pearl and three-inch legs decorated with opaque turquoise. Not long ago these pieces were shown as a side exhibit at the Queen's Gallery. Here were some of the fabulous Russian Easter eggs of gold and diamonds made for the Czar and Czarina. Here, too, was an amusing little eastern god in rose quartz, nodding his head and swaying his hands at a touch.

Some of the choice specimens of the Queen's family collection of gold boxes have also been seen, historic mementos as they are of days gone by. The monarchs of old used to give gold boxes as gifts to foreign princes or diplomats, and the jewellers who constructed these souvenirs delighted in the rarity or texture of the precious stones selected to adorn them. Some of the smaller boxes were used for snuff, and there is one box fitted with compartments with miniature toilet accessories which probably formed part of the travel kit of Queen Charlotte, the consort of George III. Queen Elizabeth II also has boxes of Staffordshire and Battersea enamel, as well as some of the tiny mysterious cases of Chelsea porcelain in which our great-great-grandmamas kept their bodkins. Then there are examples of piqué-work, tortoiseshell decorated with patterns executed in gold or silver pins.

Needless to say, the Queen's enamels, cameos, mosaics and similar bibelots are kept well away from the new heating radiators at Windsor Castle so that their delicate surfaces may come to no harm.

The fragrant custom of collecting scent bottles has passed somewhat out of fashion. Yet here again the Queen has perfume flasks in porcelain, rock crystal, ivory, agate and so on, some dating back to the eighteenth century. There are also the Chinese jades and crystals bequeathed by Queen Mary, the richly jewelled seals and fobs that go back to George IV . . . so many marvels of every kind.

A lady in waiting once gave Queen Victoria "A lovely little crown of precious stones", as she noted in her diary. It turned out to be a musical box which would play God Save the Queen, and our Queen has it still. Specially precious, too, is a musical box in the form of a gold scent flask, which was made by Parisian craftsmen and also belonged to Queen Charlotte.

Whenever the Queen has guests new to Windsor, she discovers their special interest and has some intriguing curio to show them. A Swiss visitor was naturally interested in watches. The Queen placed in his hand a cherry of red enamel; the dewdrop clinging to the stem was a diamond. And within this inviting case was an enamelled gold watch set in diamonds, a wonderful instance of ninteenth century Swiss artistry. The watch once belonged to the Queen's great-grandmother Queen Alexandra—but apparently it never succeeded in improving her notorious unpunctuality.

Early in her friendship with Lord Snowdon's mother, the Countess of Rosse, the Queen similarly discovered that they share an interest in old fans. The Queen still treasures the eighteenth century fans that gave such joy to Queen Mary. An Italian fan of carved ivory, painted with chinoiseries, and an array of French fans are among her notable examples. Such trifles play tricks with time when one may open a painted fan that perhaps fluttered under the eyes of Marie Antoinette at Versailles!

Probably the least-known of all the Queen's assembly of bibelots is the collection of her father's cigarette-cases. On royal tours it often seemed safe to reception committees to present King George VI with a cigarette-case: a beautiful if medically ill-omened treasure in ribbed gold or platinum, silver or even crystal. Today the cases are already period pieces, fast becoming rare and curious as the snuff-boxes, patch-boxes and tea-caddies of the past.

The Queen's bibelots are inexhaustible in interest. Picture to yourself the charm of a miniature tea service wrought in amber on a doll-size tray, or the tempting allurement of an apple which proves on closer sight to be a travelling set of smaller toilet articles in Meissen porcelain. Pendants, plaques, caskets, ornamental keys, even the Fabergé clock of engraved rock crystal that always stood on George V's desk . . .

The Dolls

There were no fanfares when an exhibition of the Queen's dolls opened at Windsor Castle. In the past two or three years, however, thousands of children have found an enchanting extra show when visiting the Queen's Dolls' House. In the past, when wishing to inspect that superb miniature built for Queen Mary, the public had to pass down an uninteresting corridor alongside the Castle post office. Now they leave the exhibition through a dazzling avenue of dolls.

There are dolls that both the Queen and Princess Margaret dearly loved when they were very young, and more recent dolls belonging to Princess Anne. There are scores of dolls, too, in colourful national costume presented to the Queen on overseas tours . . . and dolls that Prince Philip evidently brought home for his young family from as far away as Peru.

Many of the dolls are souvenirs of historic occasions, like the Dutch doll in clogs, lace cap and striped apron presented to the Queen during her State Visit to the Netherlands and the two little dairymaids, clasping imitation Danish cheeses, that recall the earlier visit to Denmark. When the Queen visited Lille and Roubaix in industrial France, the working folk felt that they could not compete with the glitter of Paris, but they held their own by giving the Queen three peasant dolls of their district. A girl doll in traditional Welsh costume, with red cloak and high-pointed black hat, is as charming a memento as one could wish of a royal visit to Wales.

With a mother's common sense, the Queen does not burden children with facts that only grown-ups might wish to know. So the royal dolls hold court at Windsor with only place-names at their feet, and an occasional word on ownership to help settle any family discussion.

Two bob-haired almond-eyed Japanese dolls, dressed in brilliantly flowered kimonos, hold a special pride of place, for we are told that they belonged to the Queen as a child. Yet your guess is as good as mine if you decide that the nearby doll from Hong Kong might have been a recent Christmas gift from the Duke and Duchess of Kent. Although no royal visits have been paid to Korea, an enigmatically smiling doll from that far country has found her way into the collection.

Nearly all the 150 dolls are standing magically on their own feet, as royal dolls should. Flawless craftsmanship created such poise. A group of graceful sari-clad Indians stand in the rapt absorption of a dance, and their exquisite beauty and balance is shared by an adjoining group of Pakistani ladies, posing in gorgeous gold-flecked saris, perfect even to their painted nails.

Have you ever seen a doll wearing genuine jewellery? A European doll, wearing a locket of solid gold and dressed in a pretty frock of sprigged muslin, was given to Princess Anne one year. A princess doll from Malaya, endowed with jewelled ear-rings and lovely jewel-studded bracelets and necklets, was given to the Queen. And even the proud boy doll accompanying her wears an exotic diamond or two glittering in his embroidered robes.

Visiting this sumptuous doll show, one realises indeed how readily royal children get acquainted with foreign lands—when they are still very young. At the age of five Prince Andrew could readily recognise the uniform of the Canadian North-West Mounted Police from a uniformed doll, in red jacket and blue breeches, complete even to a miniature police whistle, that long kept guard over a nursery showcase. The Mountie doll moreover is partnered by a girl doll in the brown linen frock of a social service group.

A boy doll from Greenland is warmly clad in his trappers' furs and must have travelled many miles on his snowshoes. A Red

Indian doll in magnificent feathered head-dress and flamboyant blanket is rightly accompanied by his squaw, perfect in miniature from her plaited hair to her moccasins.

No less distinctive from sunnier climes is a grass-skirted doll from Fiji and a lady in the ankle-length robes of Sierra Leone. A Ghana doll is clad with great dignity as a tribal chief. His wife in a green and orange blanket typically carries her own baby doll on her back.

Clearly not all these superbly costumed creatures can have known the hot grasp of nursery fingers. Some royal dolls are obviously made only for the sheer entertainment value of being looked at. The Queen was concerned because so few people could enjoy her Polish harvest festival. Now if you visit Windsor you will find it at a focal point of the exhibition. No fewer than twenty-four dolls, boy and girl together, gaily march in couples behind a horse-drawn market cart, looking for all the world like a set of Polish folk dancers with their decorated head-dresses and bright-coloured costumes. It hardly matters that the mettlesome horses are only made of straw.

Other dolls, only to be looked at, have become historical rarities. A wax doll in rich Highland costume was a favourite with Queen Victoria's children, and you will be charmed by two dolls mounted on a tandem bicycle that delighted the Queen's father, King George VI, when he was a little boy. In turn-of-the-century costumes, the girl has bicycling bloomers, and the boy wears doggy sporting clothes.

Another of the late King's treasures is a French mechanical doll, in the chef's cap and apron of a pastry-cook, quite capable of nodding his head, and selling brioches and sweetmeats off his tray.

Yet perhaps after all, the best royal dolls are the ones that have been used. Two very special dolls, "France" and "Marianne", were presented to the Queen and Princess Margaret when they were children, and must have led a very full and fashionable life before they were at last discarded. A sparkling blonde with roses in her hair, France at present wears a pink flowered dress with pink matching gloves on her perfectly modelled hands.

Many happy nursery hours were spent merely changing her toilette, for France has no fewer than ten extra sets of gloves of different shades in an elegant Gant Perrin box, plus floral *boutonniéres*, beaded handbags, bead necklaces and brooches, fans, a white silk sunshade, and indeed anything that a doll—or a little girl—could desire. The tortoiseshell toilet set alone is quite a marvel of elegance, with its hairbrush, comb, clothes-brush, mirror and pin jar.

Marianne is equally ready to face all the demands of a doll's day, even to her own writing pad of notepaper with her monogram "M". It says much for this little brunette's Paris couturier that her ocelot fur coat, with its matching trimmed cap and muff, seems quite fashionable today.

For summer wear Marianne can delve into her wardrobe trunk for a sailor suit; for a rainy day she has two umbrellas in blue or green, and she has a silk bedjacket for bedtime. She is the fortunate possessor, too, of three extra pairs of made-to-measure shoes, though Marianne hardly looks the kind of doll to do much walking.

A complete palace with everything reduced to one twelfth of actual size, Queen Mary's Dolls' House has, of course, no actual doll of its own. But just in case the miniature chatelaine should return unexpectedly, the Queen has knitted a gossamer bedjacket, precisely to scale, that hangs on a bathroom chair.

Curtains and carpets are cleaned, and the tiny pieces of household linen washed when necessary. Not long ago the Queen noticed that one of the pinpoint chair-legs might scratch the mother-of-pearl parquet and carefully moved it on to the carpet.

The promise of another showcase of dolls serves to lure the children from this entrancing model. There is an array of some of Queen Victoria's dolls, little ladies of about eight inches high, elegantly dressed in the furs, flounces and feathers of the 1820s. They stand among their own furniture or sit against delicately embroidered cushions, proving they can bend their arms or legs, and you will scarcely suspect that their well-kept complexions are merely painted wood. A figure from the realm of fairytale is a cork-faced old pedlar woman in a poke bonnet, with her tray of trinkets. Among her wares are tiny bracelets and the smallest dolls of all, hardly half an inch long.

The Queen's exhibition concludes with a woman-to-woman whisper that any mother will catch. As a last glimpse, children are enchanted by one of Queen Victoria's dearest treasures, a sweet little white satin cradle of twins. The two identical babies are home-made twists of rag. The cradle has been made from a cardboard box.

The best-loved dolls can be made at home!

The Queen's Clocks

A romantically bearded young man has become a familiar figure at Buckingham Palace, moving unattended and unwatched from room to room, with none of the Palace apartments denied to him. Everyone at the Palace knows Mr Potter, intent and absorbed as he moves quietly about his work, always with an eye on the time.

His firm has been caring for the royal clocks for over 100 years, and Mr Potter tends this wonderful collection of timepieces today with a measure of paternal care and affection as if they were his children.

Indeed, I first met Mr Potter when he was standing in front of the Queen's celebrated "Negress Head" clock, staring into her eyes with rapt attention. He gave a familiar tweak to her right ear-ring and her eyelids fluttered to reveal the time in the pupils, the hour in numerals in the left eye, the minutes in the right. The clock represents the head of an African princess, two-thirds life size, and the dusky lady not only tells the time in her glance but her left ear-ring is also a key to a sixteen-pipe organ which plays eight different tunes. Usually this "African Princess" adorns the 1844 Room, where she pleasantly winks at the Queen's luncheon guests. Recently, however, she visited Paris to be displayed in an exhibition and Mr Potter found that the journey upset her delicate balance. It was months before the Negress Head Clock was accurate to the minute again, and I last saw her at Windsor Castle.

Another special clock that needs watching, so to speak, is the four-faced astronomical clock first placed in the then Buckingham House in 1765. The timepiece almost presages the computer age in complexity, for the four dials not only show the time, name the days of the week and months of the year, but they also disclose the age and phases of the moon and show the motion of the planets and the time of high tide at thirty-two different ports!

Altogether the Queen has over 300 clocks at Buckingham Palace alone. There are staid old grandfathers—properly known as long-case and pedestal clocks—and delightful bracket chimers, clocks in tortoiseshell and intricate ormolu, classical timepieces in bronze and marble and delectable French clocks overflowing with sculptured figures and delicate porcelain flowers.

One monumental grandfather, nine feet two inches high, deserves to be mentioned, for it stood in the Palace of Versailles before the French Revolution and probably struck the hours for Marie Antoinette. More personal still is a little silver-gilt clock at Windsor decorated with true lovers' knots and bearing the initials H and A which was given by Henry VIII to Anne Boleyn on her wedding morning. It should perhaps have stopped for ever when she was executed only four years later but, truth to tell, the clock still keeps perfect time.

Far from being in the family all these years, one must also add that it was re-discovered and bought at a country-house auction in the present century—and actually secured by a final bid of only five shillings.

One of the 360 clocks at Windsor Castle is built into the lacy gold carving of a pier-glass, and a clock similarly built into the dining-room marble mantelpiece was faced with particularly legible figures so that Queen Victoria could always read it in her short-sighted old age.

As one might expect, the royal collection includes several superb clocks by Thomas Tompion, the blacksmith's son who became "the father of English clock-making" in the reign of Charles II and was ultimately buried in Westminster Abbey. The Queen's finest Tompion is a signed oak and walnut longcase that shows the day of the week and the day of the month and goes for a year without winding. Visitors also always admire a charming Tompion bracket-clock that belonged to Queen Mary, and they are occasionally deceived by a round clockface that proves in reality to be a Tompion wheeled barometer of about the year 1680. It is astonishing to realize that some of these clocks have been keeping time for 300 years and yet remain in perfect order today.

Undoubtedly the Queen's best-loved clock also belonged to her favourite character in family history, seven reigns away from our own time, the modest and unassuming Queen Charlotte.

Seen in the Zoffany portrait of Queen Charlotte with two of her sons, this piece is a true charmer, a small highly decorative French longcase clock of the type so often described as a grandmother. With a touch of sentiment, it softly ticks away the hours in a corridor of Windsor Castle, keeping guard beside Queen Charlotte's beautiful old jewel cabinet. The Zoffany painting hangs nearby and in the right-hand background of the picture one can see the clock, looking exactly the same then as now.

Queen Charlotte also liked to match her clocks with door-handles, wall-brackets and other accessories and, as I mentioned earlier, a pair of her Chelsea china mantel clocks at Buckingham Palace, decorated by painted figures of a shepherd and shepherdess, suggest the floral charm of her eighteenth century living-room. And still there are other fine old clocks one should mention, including a rare timepiece in the form of a temple that bears the date 1598 and was made for Queen Elizabeth the First.

There are estimated to be 250 clocks at Balmoral and 160 at Sandringham, perhaps more than 1,000 clocks in all the royal homes. What a mellow and pleasant orchestral sound it would be if they could all be heard chiming together!

One of the Palace musical clocks offers a selection of popular airs that specially endeared it to the Queen's grandfather, King George V. After striking the hour it plays four tunes, with matching tunes played for every quarter-hour. Old singing-bird clocks are said to be particularly fragile, although the Queen has two still in full song at Sandringham. At Buckingham Palace, too, I imagine that no one is surprised at hearing the call of the cuckoo months out of season, for a cuckoo clock was presented to the Queen some years ago and still holds a place of honour in the nursery. Instead of the traditional Swiss chalet, however, an English tudor cottage contains the clock, and the little grey and blue cuckoo both opens its beak and bows.

If you could have any of the rich and ornate royal clocks to keep you company through the day, which would you choose? The Queen in reality prefers her wrist-watch, of 18-carat gold and with a 17-jewel movement, the smallest ever made in Britain. This was presented to her after she had lost, to her great distress, an equally tiny French platinum watch in the snow at Sandringham. Despite every search, this was never found, and it may still lie somewhere in the fields as treasure-trove for the future.

Obviously, there is no tactful opportunity to glance at her watch while receiving visitors, and so on her desk Her Majesty keeps one of the oldest clocks of all, an hour-glass with which she unobtrusively times an audience as the sand drifts from top to bottom.

The Queen's Keepsakes

Enhancing the new contemporary atmosphere of all the royal palaces one may recognize treasures that were not there when the Queen first came to the throne, beautiful things in gold and silver, crystal and porcelain, ebony and jade, adding their own enriching significance to the present-day milieu of the Royal Family.

These are the gifts that the Queen and her husband have brought back with them from their travels, the souvenirs of State Visits, mementos of strengthened or new-forged friendships, objects of intrinsic beauty and interest from all over the world. An exchange of gifts has always been one of the happiest traditional ceremonies of a State Visit. When the Queen visited Italy, for instance, she was given a rare and lovely seventeenth century clock by Mercanti, one of the greatest Italian clock-makers. And when the 1969 visit of the President of Italy to Windsor was first planned, the Queen at once decided that the clock should be placed in his suite in a timely token of welcome.

Some people imagine that all the gifts the Queen receives overseas are brought home and placed in a vast store-room at Windsor Castle but no such room exists. The fact is that the Queen likes to see her keepsakes about her, or so placed—as with an object of art—that they continually conjure up remembrance and inspiration.

On one of her desks she regularly uses the hand-carved pencil tray and other items from the ivory desk set given to her by the President of the Sudan—an active reminder indeed of diplomatic difficulties that friendship between two Heads of State helped to smooth away. On another desk her notepaper is kept in a sandalwood case unexpectedly given to her during the tour of India when she visited Mysore. On a silver-inlaid writing table at Windsor the Queen uses a silver-embossed leather desk set presented to her in Portugal . . . and elsewhere a sumptuous ink-stand and pen-tray is made of British Columbian gold and silver, a happy souvenir of a visit to Victoria.

In her study at Buckingham Palace, the Queen keeps a notable bronze of a negro head by the Nigerian sculptor, Ben Enwonwu, in token of the problems of all her varied Commonwealth peoples. And one might mention a crystal paperweight from Stockholm, a silver paper-knife from Santiago and an exquisite jewelled photograph frame from Belgium . . . reminders all within the Queen's daily working orbit.

The Queen indeed exercises considerable care, blended with tact and sentiment, in deciding where a gift to her would be best kept. The Mayor of Venice presented her with a bronze replica of his city symbol, the Lion of Venice, and it now stands on an Italian side-table in the main corridor of Windsor Castle close to a magnificent Canaletto painting of the Grand Canal. The Bavarian government gave the Queen a rare if somewhat large blue and gold vase of eighteenth century Nymphenburg porcelain. Now it flanks a Windsor portrait of Prince Albert, whose boyhood home was full of fine Nymphenburg.

Experts in protocol naturally cudgel their brains to select gifts that will fulfil a royal need while reminding the Queen of the donor. Mayor Willy Brandt of West Berlin discovered that there are few German clocks in the royal collection and he chose an ideal memento in a beautiful clock dated 1766 from the Berlin Porcelain Manufactory. The Mayor of Bonn rivalled this originality, for his city gave the Queen records of all the symphonies of Beethhoven, Bonn's most famous son.

When the Shah of Persia gave the Queen a sumptuous vanity case of inlaid walnut with bottles mounted in gold filligree, she promised enthusiastically, "I will take it wherever I go," and sure enough the case invariably accompanies her on the royal yacht *Britannia*. A silk carpet from the Shah has similarly found a perfect setting in the Silk Tapestry Room at Buckingham Palace, and every summer some of the first-cut Palace roses are always placed in an inscribed rose bowl that was a gift from President Jonas of Austria.

At every point in the Queen's environment, in fact, one finds these symbols of people and places and of duties done. A cavalcade of white porcelain horses in a personal display cabinet were a gift from Mrs Jonas. On the other side of the room, a set of delectable child figurines in Royal Copenhagen porcelain remain as a memento of the Queen's State Visit to Denmark.

Naturally, these were a present to Prince Philip as well, for the interests of husband and wife can seldom be separated. A barefoot statuette of the Queen, carved with primitive Eskimo artistry from green serpentine rock and whalebone, is an important decorative element in his personal apartments. A tapestry carpet portrait of the Queen, from Persia, hung on his walls for a time and visitors often admire a medieval miniature of Oriental princes playing polo without realizing it was a perfectly chosen gift from Germany.

In America, too, President Eisenhower once gave the Queen a ceramic sculpture of her husband as a polo-player. Then, with a twinkle, he announced that he would also like his guests to accept a picture "by a supreme artist" . . . and the extra present turned out to be a very good portrait of the young Prince Charles painted by the President himself.

The importance of gifts in the goodwill between nations can be seen in the fact that the flower-painted overmantel in the State Dining Room at the White House was part of an exchange of presents when the Queen was still Princess Elizabeth. Back in 1957 the royal couple gave the Eisenhowers an exquisite porcelain model of a pair of American warbler birds, and in 1964 the Queen received from Washington a similarly sculptured porcelain model of the thrush-like American robin, an enchanting piece posed against early Spring flowers.

The list of presentations could be endless. Mounted on gold as a paperweight, a stack of pieces of eight from a sunken galleon form a romantic souvenir of the Bahamas. But there is a Nigerian tiger-paw paperweight at Sandringham, and a remarkable paperweight made of Alberta dinosaur bone is in use at Balmoral!

A visitor was once surprised to see the Queen driving a Renault in Windsor Great Park, but the French-made car was in fact given to her during her State Visit to France. Her opulent fur-backed car rug was a gift from the President of Chile. Diamonds glistened at the Queen's lapel and it may well be that she was wearing her fern-leaf diamond brooch from New Zealand.

The Queen's personal jewellery, of course, glitters richly in keepsakes. They range from the bracelet and necklet of the diamonds given her in South Africa on her coming-of-age to the Brazilian necklace of diamonds and aquarmarines, a Coronation gift, which she significantly wore in Brazil only last year. The Emperor Haile Selassie of Ethiopia gave the Queen a Red Sea pearl necklace, spilling magnificently from an open jewel box. King Faisal of Saudi Arabia presented a diamond and platinum necklace that drew a gasp of sheer wonderment . . .

A special quality of these gifts is often in the surprise element. Royal secretaries, when asked to hint at presents that might be welcome, are apt to suggest that a gift need not be expensive. When the children were younger, the Queen was always happy to accept a doll, preferably dressed in local costume, and a delightful exhibition of the Queen's dolls—which is open to the public—has thrilled thousands of young visitors to Windsor.

The Queen herself also likes to see souvenirs of her travels in the homes of her friends. In Venice, on one occasion, she window-shopped perceptively while hemmed in by huge crowds. Later, when all was quiet, her dresser went out to purchase the pieces she had noticed. After the Queen returns home from an overseas visit, a Customs officer calls at Buckingham Palace. The Queen's gifts and purchases ready for his inspection and, by her own wish, Her Majesty pays duty and purchase tax like any other traveller.

Only the presentations officially made to her as a Head of State are exempt. It would be difficult to assess the value of some of the wonderful souvenirs of her eastern travels—silver models of Indian temples, a gold replica of a chief's palanquin from Ghana. One may wonder what place there is for these exotic treasures in sombre London. All are carefully tended, however, by the yeomen of the gold and silver pantries at Buckingham Palace, ready for use as a possible centrepiece of a State banquet to an appropriate Eastern or African guest.

The Queen has a display cabinet of City keys and a wallcase devoted to scrolls of welcome. Nowadays she is known to prefer that generosity should be diverted to the provision of scholarships, the endowment of hospitals and other good works. In lieu of a gift, for example, Bonn University now gives an annual Queen Elizabeth prize to the best student of English. Newfoundland has utilised gift money for an assistance scheme for retarded children. Instead of jewels, both Ontario and British Columbia have instituted lavish scholarship funds. These are permanent souvenirs which we all seem to share.

11 Prince Philip's Paintings

A legend persists that the Queen's husband knows little of art. In fact, he is a lively patron of artists and a discerning purchaser.

Invited into Prince Philip's library and workroom at Buckingham Palace, nervous newcomers are often surprised when they find that the chief note of decoration is a semi-abstract modernist painting. The room is pleasantly contemporary with its low-slung sofas and easy-chairs; and the painting seems to reflect the browns of the fabrics, the softly-lit deep gold of the ceiling, and indeed to express Prince Philip's own restless personality.

Then one sees that the work represents two horses' heads, truly a picture for a man's room, vigorously original in style. It is in fact "Primavera" by Myriam d'Acceglio. As it happens, I cannot find anyone who knows anything of d'Acceglio, nor can the Duke of Edinburgh's staff enlighten me. It would accord with H.R.H.'s reputation if the painting were by himself or an amateur artist among his friends.

At Windsor Castle, however, guests are invariably taken aback by a vehement abstract painting by Alan Davie and there is no doubt about this identity. Controversial in its primary colours and forceful pattern, the Queen and Prince Philip jointly chose the picture for their home before the artist had even decided on its title and the unframed canvas was labelled merely "No. 19".

A visit to the Palace of Holyroodhouse, in Edinburgh, produces more surprises, for here the dull corridors and sombre private apartments are unexpectedly enlivened by scores of modern paintings and drawings. A brilliant selection, mainly of the work of fifty young Scottish artists, the effect is electric in this ancient Scottish home.

But those who often decry Prince Philip's patronage of the arts should know that each and every picture has been bought by the Queen's husband from his own private funds.

The Queen recently purchased an eighteenth century portrait of Bonnie Prince Charlie for Holyroodhouse. In contrast, the Duke of Edinburgh's contribution is astringent and unorthodox. Ranging from unconventional and effective landscapes—there's one entitled "View of Back Gardens"—to way-out still lifes and present-day portraits, the collection represents his own distinctive choice. He once toured a Royal Scottish academy exhibition, flecking his catalogue with pencil-notes, and next morning ordered twelve paintings by telephone.

Prince Philip shows a keenly realistic approach in his cash encouragement of young artists. Yet the legend persists that he knows nothing of art and regards all contemporary experiment as a joke. Headlines blazoned his sallies at the expense of a Henry Moore sculpture, though in reality the Prince was trying to amuse and "soften up" an awed schoolboy audience. Nearly every newspaper reported his irrepressible wisecrack, "Who perpetrated that?" at the sight of an enigmatic abstract painting. Many of us find amusement as well as stimulus in much recent art, and prefer wit to pomposity. Prince Philip once quipped, "Goodness, look what they're asking for it!" confronting a high-priced piece of modern sculpture. And yet he proudly owns a no-doubt equally expensive symbolic oil-painting by Graham Sutherland, a mysterious composition of twining tendrils and exotic forms.

William Dobell, the Australian artist, received a knighthood in a recent Honours list. Prince Philip was most impressed with his paintings when, as a young naval lieutenant in Sydney just after the war, he spent an afternoon of his precious shore leave visiting a Dobell exhibition.

The Prince felt that he had no money to spend on pictures in those days, but more recently he gave Dobell a commission for two works. "Paint whatever you like!" he suggested . . . rare and encouraging patronage for any artist. Today two valuable Dobell pictures, "Beach Scene" and "Country Fair", hang in Prince Philip's private apartments.

It was the same with Edward Seago, the Norfolk artist, whose chill-blue oil-painting, "Icebergs at Base W", is one of several Seago pictures on Prince Philip's walls. Here was an enthusiasm no doubt acquired from the Queen Mother, who has four of five more homely Seago studies at Clarence House. Admiration took a practical form, for the Prince invited the artist to join him on the Royal yacht *Britannia's* cruise to the Antarctic, painting as he pleased.

The two men got to know one another as only shipboard companions can. "The Duke is an amazing man who longs to be knowledgeable about everything," Mr Seago summed up afterwards. And perhaps this is the clue to Prince Philip's misunderstood zest and discernment. He would be the first to admit that he knew little of the arts in the days when, as plain Lieut. Philip Mountbatten, R.N., he became engaged to the then Princess Elizabeth. The first picture he ever commissioned, in fact, was a portrait miniature of his bride.

The collection of miniatures at Sandringham hinted that this was the ideal form for an intimate portrait for desk or mantelshelf, or for a young officer to take to sea when he resumed his naval career. Naturally the miniature had to be painted by the finest artist specialising in the field, and Prince Philip typically sought advice of the royal art expert, the late Sir James Mann.

There ensued a cloak-and-dagger episode for Stella Marks, whose miniature portraits are so well known. Sir James borrowed some of her works to show to a mysterious friend and subsequently, of course, the present Queen gave Mrs Marks a series of sittings. The miniature, a water-colour painted on ivory, is still Prince Philip's greatest treasure, and Stella Marks eventually painted all the members of the Royal Family.

When the Queen and her husband were first married, the young couple received over sixty paintings and drawings among their wedding gifts, pictures by Wilson Steer, Paul Nash, Feliks Topolski and many others, the nucleus of a highly personal collection. When the Duke of Edinburgh felt that it was time to launch out as a collector, he decided to start by collecting the original drawings of newspaper cartoons and before long he had a lively framed collection of some of the best works of Low, Giles, Strube, Osbert Lancaster and others.

In Malta he discovered that two local artists, the Apap brothers, were having a lot of sideline fun in producing little caricature statuettes. Prince Philip commissioned eight figures and named the personalities he wished to see caricatured—and so Earl Mountbatten, Field-Marshal Montgomery, Lord Avon, Sir Winston Churchill and the Archbishop of Canterbury, among others, joined the amusing royal collection. But William Apap was also a serious painter, and Prince Philip speedily commissioned a portrait of Princess Anne, while the sculptor brother, Vincent, was asked for a bronze head of Prince Charles.

It might be said that the Queen's husband knows what he likes . . . and consistently strives to enlarge the horizon of what he knows. At the opening crush of the memorable Picasso exhibition at the Tate Gallery, it was noted that the Prince stayed only half an hour. In reality, he avoided the crowds another evening when the gallery was officially closed and stayed all evening discussing the pictures with his friends.

Characteristically, Prince Philip took up landscape painting as a hobby, teaching himself to grapple at first hand with the artist's problems of technique. No doubt with something of the awe with which anyone would show his own amateur work to a distinguished artist, he hesitantly showed some canvases to Annigoni for a critical opinion, and the Italian maestro said that he found a grasp and force unusual in a beginner. Very few people have seen these personal royal paintings, but they are said to be confident and impressionist in Churchill style.

The Prince rarely visits a modern art exhibition without buying something when pictures are for sale. He once visited a show at the Royal Society of Painters in Water Colours and noticed the work of one of the youngest members, Alan Carr Linford. Then he bought four etchings by Mr Linford for the private rooms of the royal yacht *Britannia* and later he commissioned twenty-four water colours of Windsor scenes. The royal record for instant patronage occurred at a Scottish Academy summer exhibition when no fewer than eighteen red labels indicating a sale appeared on pictures shortly after Prince Philip had strolled around.

The diplomats, cabinet ministers and others privileged to enter Buckingham Palace through the broad southern corridor—the Right of Entrée—are vividly confronted with proof of his distinctive and sometimes satiric taste. The corridor used to be a portrait gallery of stern old admirals interspersed with varnished sea battles. The Queen's husband personally commissioned Feliks Topolski to paint a procession of eight huge panels depicting the Coronation, an exhilarating 100-feet mural of spidery irreverence and fun.

We must hope that we may all one day enjoy the extraordinary verve of this work, perhaps at the Queen's Gallery. And, indeed, nearly five years of successful exhibitions have been held since it was officially announced that the idea of creating the Gallery came from both the Queen *and* her husband.

THE CIRCUMSTANCE

12 The Queen's Mail

A sensitive barometer of loyalty, a clearing-house of human problems, a court of last appeal...

Nothing measures the popularity of the Monarchy more than the daily variety of mail that crosses the Queen's desk—from the avalanche of good wishes for birthdays and Christmas (which the small royal staff cannot always acknowledge) to the problem letters, which are always answered.

On the occasion of a special anniversary, or after a successful overseas royal tour, the court postmaster, Leslie Butters, clocks some 1,600 incoming "messages" a day, apart from ordinary administrative palace mail. The birth of Prince Andrew brought a record influx of 5,000 telegrams alone and incoming mail was also significantly heavy in the week following the first informal radio broadcast made by the Prince of Wales.

Outward-bound, the inner contents of the Queen's personal mail remain top-secret for posterity. The Queen seals her own letters in opaque envelopes with dark-grey linings, proof against probing lamplight and prying eyes. The precaution is mainly against accidents in transit, for all the Queen's personal correspondents of course shield her secrets with scrupulous care.

Our children will probably have to wait until sometime next century to learn how the sympathy and encouragement of Queen Elizabeth's letters helped lift Jacqueline Kennedy from the dark gulfs of widowhood, or how the Queen's shared practical experience helped her find the aura of everyday privacy that led to her happy second marriage with Aristotle Onassis.

After the assassination of Dr Verwoerd in South Africa, there was criticism that the Queen, on the advice of her ministers, had not sent an official message to his widow. Only the injustice of the storm stung Mrs Verwoerd into revealing that the Queen had, in fact, written "private letters full of kindness and consolation".

Until recently the world similarly knew nothing of the Queen's long historic thank-you letter to Sir Winston Churchill, when she learned that his retirement was certain. Sir Winston's physician, Lord Moran, tore open that chink in the royal notepaper curtain when he published his journals. "I had a lovely letter from her," Winston had confided one day. "Eight pages in her own writing. It took me a whole morning to reply."

In her own environment the Queen is recognized indeed as a considerable letter-writer, endowed with inherited talent and ranking with the royal letter-writers of history. She was trained to regard this task as a pleasure in childhood, and letters she wrote at age eleven were already vivid with detail. "The march past of 4,600 soldiers was very tiring because we stood for over an hour and dust continually blowing in our eyes," she incisively described a military pageant. More recently, I have seen the Queen's own tender view of one of her babies, "Actually he has got an interesting pair of hands for a baby . . . rather large, but fine with long fingers—quite unlike mine and certainly unlike his father's . . ."

Queen Victoria might have read such words with beaming pleasure but, protected by a hierarchy of courtiers and secretaries, she surely could not have been reached by the letters that come direct to our own Queen: "Your Majesty, I am writing as woman to woman in regard to my husband . . . sentenced to ten years' imprisonment . . . I am going mad with worry . . ." Or, a desperately sick man borrows a sheet of paper to tell her of his "mountain of debts . . . the children with scarcely a stitch to their backs."

Stiff with human problems, the royal-mail influx has doubled since George VI's reign. In the busy post office in Buckingham Palace, the court postmaster's team now numbers twelve, with two staff in addition in permanent residence at Windsor Castle. The royal postmen wear a distinctive breast badge on their uniform and transfer to Balmoral or Sandringham as required. Their task, of course, is merely to sort and dispatch mail to all the royal departments, but the Queen insists that every letter addressed to her shall go to her first of all.

Postmaster Butters takes up her post himself in wicker baskets and the Queen makes a point of always glancing over it by 9 a.m. When her secretaries sort and classify the letters, many can be dealt with by standing instructions, such as the acknowledgement of birthday greetings or a reply to criticisms that have run to routine pattern. Yet the morning mail is never cleared without many a précis to the Queen, and a large daily batch of letters always requires her special decision.

The Private Secretary, Sir Michael Adeane, usually goes to her promptly at ten o'clock with correspondence on every matter of state or protocol, from an invitation to a state visit or special letters from perhaps her Commonwealth Prime Ministers. Next, the Assistant Private Secretary, Sir Martin Charteris, formerly of Middle East military intelligence, helps the Queen handle correspondence involving her everyday official activities and letters from the public. If she has been asked to launch a liner or visit a hospital, Charteris has possible dates and schedules at his fingertips. If a painter has suggested a new theme for a royal art exhibition, Charteris collects the views of royal art advisers before he seeks the Queen's answer.

The Queen's other Assistant Private Secretary, ex-bomber pilot Philip Moore, began his duties by dealing with domestic household matters. "You will find they are mainly routine," he was told. Yet soon he was coping with two Iron Curtain refugees who wrote asking if they could become housemaids at Sandringham. The Queen assented, and after security checks they got jobs.

Her Majesty is adept at going briskly through long foolscap lists of questions, expressing her decisions with a pencil tick or a word or two, and she takes pride in keeping abreast of the work every day. Not long ago, when time-and-motion experts were invited to work-study and if possible streamline Palace efficiency, it was suggested that they should begin with the secretariat and correspondence. The investigators doubtfully trudged up winding stone stairways to the mezzanine floor where the Queen's nine clerks and shorthand-typists work in rooms better soundproofed than modern office buildings. Some take notebook dictation from Adeane or

Charteris, while others work from Prince Philip's dictation tapes. Two are engaged solely in coping with the world's film and press enquiries. If the investigators had half-expected to see quill pens, they found modern electronic copying equipment. All the royal typewriters produce specially legible and permanent lettering, more forgery-proof than electric typewriters.

The efficiency experts may have cast a critical eye on the big Chippendale desk in the Queen's sitting room, crowded with family photographs, paper knives, a pastepot, an ancient hour-glass, a leather dispatch box for State papers, scribbling pads and a letter basket or two, but the Queen feels that she works best among family mementos. At her side there's an intercom link with her husband and all royal departments, an angle-lamp of ruthless efficiency, and a business-like worktable that the Queen likes to keep clear. Her other working desk, an ornate French bureau in her audience-room, where she sometimes sits to make working notes, is equally littered but purposeful.

The Queen uses several gold fountain pens, filled with ink of special permanence. Ball-points are out, chiefly because the Palace can't yet be sure that the ink never fades. Palace courtesy, too, demands that letters be at least partly answered in the signer's own hand. So "Dear Sir" or "Yours Sincerely" is usually hand-written.

Many a palace letter simply begins "Dear Tommy" or "Dear Susan". Letters from children are usually "processed," as officials say, by a lady in waiting, aided by a stenographer who works on one of the clearest largest-print typewriters in the office. The Queen gains genuine pleasure from the naïveté and charm of a child's letter and likes to think that she herself answers them. So her ladies clear any problems in a few minutes' conversation, and then take over.

A crippled schoolboy recently wrote to the Queen explaining that six major operations had saved his life and suggesting an MBE—the Beatles' honour—for his surgeon. A reply came from No. 10 Downing Street, where such honours are recommended, to say that his suggestion was receiving full consideration.

In the same vein, a trade-union secretary wrote to the Queen about an old stonemason thrown out of work when the restoration of the blitzed Temple Church was at long last completed. "Is it possible to give him employment on Crown property?" he enquired, and on the Queen's direct intervention the craftsman was given a job at the Tower of London. With some temerity, a young comedian wrote pointing out that the last Court jester had worn cap and bells for Elizabeth I and suggesting that Elizabeth II might revive the role. The reply—from the Lord Chamberlain's office—had to be sympathetic but firm: "I fear the unsophisticated days of court jesters are incapable of revival. There is not the slightest possibility of a new appointment ever being made."

On the other hand, it is clear that many people still regard their Queen as a last court of appeal. A farmer was troubled by plans for a new motorway over his land and so spent his winter evenings composing "a petition of justice". Faced with eviction, a Norfolk mother of eight invoked the Queen's help in finding a house. Inevitably such letters spell longer hours and a rising backlog of work to the actually very small working staff at Buckingham Palace.

A group of London schoolboys have petitioned for more pay for teachers and members of the Young Communist League handed in a letter, saying that the Palace could house 1,000 homeless Londoners. (One may visualize Henry Moore sketching the future sleepers in the State Apartments.)

Incidentally, one of the Queen's postmen, a keen philatelist, confesses that his fingers itch for some of the strange stamps on letters from every quarter of the globe. The Queen's wonderful royal collection of stamps nowadays concerns only unused mint issues or rare "first covers", but the best used specimens are thoughtfully recovered from the day's mail and sent to a charity.

Postmarks, too, tell a tale. Some of the pathetically regular correspondents are patients in mental hospitals, and more than one senior Palace clerk can readily detect every habitual writer of this type by the eccentric handwriting alone. A lunatic fringe appears to consider conspiratorial subterfuge necessary in approaching the Queen. One insistent petitioner evidently has the use of seven different typewriters but his customary postmark gives him away.

The Queen's private letters from family and friends bear the initials of the senders or some other readily recognized sign on the envelope. (Strangers who attempt to gain priority with fake initials invariably fail.) Writing on exclusive "Original Turkey Mill Kent," a thick white plain-edged notepaper used throughout the palaces, the Queen similarly initials her own personal letters E.R. on the corner of the envelope. She addresses the envelope herself, too, and although she learned to type in her teens, her personal letters are always in her own hand.

Within Britain the Queen's personal or official letters are sent by palace messenger or registered mail. Her overseas classified mail is carried by the silver-badged Queen's Messengers, those couriers who carry all top-level Foreign Office and Commonwealth mail, and for whom a late seat is reserved on nearly every outward-bound British plane.

Not that you'll find James Bond at the door if you send Prince Edward a postcard. But your postman may deliver a thick-papered unstamped envelope with the Royal Arms on the back flap and perhaps "Windsor, Berks—Official Paid" as the postmark.

None of the Queen's letters bears postage stamps. Nor does any royal letter bear the familiar slogan "On Her Majesty's Service." Instead, there's a distinctive double-rimmed stamp of the royal cypher (E.R.) and crown.

The Queen herself insists that outward Palace mail must not seem to be stereotyped. Thousands congratulated the Queen on her fortieth birthday, and each received an individual typed acknowledgment, many slightly different in phrasing. The staff worked long hours rather than stoop to a mimeographed response. On the other hand, a heavy Christmas card crop once elicited a printed message of "thanks for the Christmas greetings you kindly sent which are heartily reciprocated". This delighted the genuine . . . but one can sense the rebuke to those inconsiderate enough to add to the Queen's working load.

Naturally, it eases the pressure that many royal letters are subsequently funnelled through government departments. A housewife protested that she had lost a big win on the football pools owing to postal delays. The Palace replied that her letter had been forwarded to the Postmaster-General. Threatened with ill-considered eviction, a group of slum-dwellers wrote to the Queen. Their letter was passed to the local housing authority for effective action.

Army regulations forbid a direct approach to the Queen but a wary old soldier carefully applied to her secretary in a pensions squabble. Seeking an equally devious intervention, another soldier objected to transfer from his regiment. The Queen actually read out his letter at an Army dinner at which she was guest of honour. "They have taken my cap badge away and with it the great love of my life. The traditions of my regiment are in my blood . . ."

Yet still the letters flood in, from anxious mothers and worried wives, from children and charities, from humble homes as well as stately. The Queen's letters have turned Buckingham Palace into a great clearing house of human hopes.

It is instructive to recall that "woman-to-woman" letter to the Queen, written in deep distress by a soldier's wife when her husband was sentenced to ten years imprisonment. The reply from a lady in waiting was swift, practical and deeply compassionate: "Her Majesty is so sorry for you in your great trouble and understands the anxiety and distress you are suffering, but I am sure you will understand that it is not possible for the Queen to intervene in matters concerning the law. I am to ask you whether you would like to talk over your troubles with a kind and understanding member of Toc H Women's section who would come to see you quite privately. Perhaps you would let me know?"

Wise and experienced counsel inevitably brought results. In another instance, a despairing mother sought the Queen's help after waiting ten months for definite news of her young soldier son, lost in the Malayan jungle. He had at first been "reported missing" and then "believed dead". The mother had vainly sought further news through every official source, and the Queen, she said, was her last resort. On Her Majesty's direct request a British Legion official got into touch with the Malay base by radio. By midday the mother knew the final tragic certainty that was better than the months of desolate hope.

It becomes noticeable that the social conditions reflected in the Queen's letters have improved throughout her reign. The abolition of capital punishment, for example, diminished the emotional strain of family appeals for reprieve. The scope of the national health services has curbed the frantic pleas from the parents of desperately sick children who often believe, against hope, that something can still be done. In an early instance, that of little Richard Buxton, a Lincolnshire farm-worker's wife was told that her six-months-old son would die of a rare disease. The Queen arranged a consultation with a top London specialist who undertook the millionth chance of an operation and the little boy's life was saved.

"How can I ever thank you?" says the mother. One hears of these cases, indeed, only from the people themselves, for no one at the Palace ever discusses the Queen's correspondence. A Sikh complained at not being allowed to wear his turban in a Glasgow ballroom, and spread the news through his community when he learned that, at the Queen's wish, local magistrates were to give their advice. A dockland parson submitted a report on the prostitution, drug-taking and squalor in his parish and said, "I don't believe the Queen would wish to be spared".

When anonymous donations poured into his funds the parson announced, "Her Majesty has acknowledged my report in a manner that reveals she is deeply concerned." An Ontario high school made 500 photostat copies of a royal reply to "loyal greetings". Australian immigrants pinned the Queen's reply on their hostel notice-board after they had complained of living conditions. Naturally, this quickly leaked to the press.

Few people can resist telling the neighbours when a letter from Buckingham Palace, with its red-embossed address heading, comes through the letterbox. And certainly whenever a royal tour is announced, both at home or overseas, always there follows a backwash of proposals that the royal car should stop near a house, farm, block of flats—and even house-boat—for the sake of an ailing child or an aged granny. A not untypical reply was sent to a Mrs Ethel Bust. "I am commanded by the Queen to acknowledge your letter and to say that Her Majesty's car will be going exremely slowly through areas where any number of her loyal subjects are assembled. I feel sure that you and your son will be able to get view of Her Majesty . . ."

When a schoolgirl asked if it would be possible to see the Queen while visiting London, the reply was that "If you could be at the Palace gates at 11 a.m. on 8 May, you would be able to see Her

Majesty." In similar letters, one of the Queen's forthcoming public engagements is named and timed and the lady in waiting adds, "Perhaps this might be an occasion to achieve your wish." One disappointed young lady wrote that the Queen had not sent a telegram of congratulation on her great-grandfather's 100th birthday. A secretary had to plead that the Palace had not been told in advance. In practice the Queen sends 1500 telegrams of congratulation for centenaries every year and will respond for diamond weddings, too.

One old lady wrote a long saga of her married life. The reply assured her of "Her Majesty's personal interest". A loyal Scotsman felt impelled to write to the Palace in praise of his wife's mother. This brought the friendly response, "The Queen was very interested to hear about your mother-in-law, who must be a wonderful old lady."

Royal lapses in mailbag efficiency are rare. A group of drama students of McKinney, Texas, were none too serious when they wrote to the Queen for a Union Jack for their school production of "H.M.S. Pinafore". A lady in waiting wrote that in response to their request the flag would arrive, and the British Embassy in Washington duly sent one along on time . . . on loan.

Though their land is now a republic, four Johannesburg girls began a letter "Dear Queen" and went on—as so many do—to express their admiration of royalty. The Queen replied that she would like to see the young ambassadors if they ever came to London. Funds for the trip were raised at a local level, officials at South Africa House were consulted and an admittedly brief meeting took place as the Queen left the Palace.

In the same way, five of the Canadian Mounted Police who had looked after the Queen were invited to London—a royal gesture to her security squad—and a child wrote to the Palace inviting the five to tea. "Mounties are my TV favourites," she explained, "and I would like to meet some real ones". The projected tea-party developed into a visit to 400 children at school. A hospital matron once apologized to the Queen when she heard that a royal visit had been unofficially suggested by two of her nursing staff. "But I was glad to hear from them," said the Queen. "I wanted to come, you know".

The Queen has never forgotten how the letters she received from children, when she was still a little girl, first gave her a sense of royal mission. "They were letters from lonely prairie farms and distant mission stations," the family friend, Lady Helen Graham, once wrote. "All breathing loyalty and affection, they brought the first direct revelation to the Princess that she was of importance to the Commonwealth."

When she married and had her own establishment, her eager helpfulness worried her staff, lest she fell prey—as Queen Alexandra often did—to the professional begging-letter writer. Doubtful cases were investigated before the then Princess knew much about them, and the bogus traders in ailing children and aged hardship were sternly warned off.

The more striking cross-samples from the Queen's early correspondence may also merit retelling. There was the Scots girl "writing as one lassie to another", fearful at a crucial moment when her "soldier-boy" did not want to marry her. Some confidential correspondence ensued with the regimental padre until a jubilant letter came, "Your Royal Highness, I am now the happiest woman in the world. My soldier has married me and I owe it all to you."

An English bride of a G.I. in Kansas City pleaded that she was unable to raise the fare to return home to see her father in what was perhaps the last year of his life. The lady in waiting replied that "enquiries are being made and you will be notified further should there be some means of helping you." The British Consul smoothed away obstacles through a philanthropic organisation.

Clarence House in those days was partly staffed by applicants who wrote for jobs out of the blue, and there are several instances of royal mail solving the staff problem. A sixteen-year-old youth named Earnest Poole notably poured into a letter his love of horses and his dreams of becoming a jockey. A job in a racing stables, he pleaded, could start him at the bottom rung of the ladder. "I know how you like horses," he ended. "You will understand how I feel." Within forty-eight hours he learned that his letter had been forwarded to the Queen's racing trainer at that time, Captain Boyd-Rochfort. Within a week he began work at the Captain's Newmarket stables. More recently, the wife of a London draughtsman wished to become a hairdresser in Mayfair but could not gain an interview with any of the big names. She ventued to write to Princess Margaret . . . and was soon an assistant with the Princess's own hairdresser.

The Duke of Edinburgh, Queen Elizabeth the Queen Mother and the Prince of Wales all have their widely different "duty mail". Even at the edge of the Arctic Circle, an Eskimo girl at Fort Simpson will never forget that she once wrote to Prince Philip inviting him to visit her community. Her township was included as an extra stop in his tour through the North-West Territories.

The Duke's forceful reputation has in turn relieved the Queen of many problems. When a young mother despaired of ever getting a children's play-ground established in her crowded industrial district, she at last wrote to Prince Philip—and his pet project, the National Playing Fields Association, of course took the matter up with the local mayor. And as the mayor himself said, "It woke everyone up. We took immediate action."

Again, the springs of quick action were tested by a carpenter's wife whose husband needed a spine operation. "I am told he must wait his turn. But if you could hear my Syd groaning in pain you would know how I feel . . ." There are, sadly, many cases in which harassed royalty cannot always intervene with success. This instance was satisfactorily settled when a leading nerve surgeon performed a successful operation shortly afterwards.

Not least, the trends of royal mail curiously reflect the public image. Both the Prince of Wales and Princess Anne receive an ever-growing mail from their own age group. The Queen Mother's mail shows a larger proportion of oldsters . . ."You won't remember me but you spoke to me before the war . . ." A member of her staff has told me, "Sometimes Queen Elizabeth gets such a nice letter that it warms everyone at Clarence House for the rest of the day . . ."

The Queen and Royal Family, in fact, relish the pleasures, the duties and the discipline of their ever-demanding mail. The Queen has never forgotten seeing the huge pyramid of messages from well-wishers piled up for her shortly before her marriage . . . and she remembers her delight when it was exceeded in volume by the letters for her parents' silver wedding a few months later. "We were both dumbfounded," her father, King George VI, wrote at the time. "We have received so many nice letters from all and sundry, thanking us for what we have tried to do . . . It does spur us on."

13 The Queen's Money

Palaces, jewels and £475,000 a year. . . . But the harsh fact remains that the Commonwealth pays the Queen nothing.

Alone among all the world's highly-paid and successful professional women, Queen Elizabeth II enjoys one special privilege, shared only perhaps by her colleague in rulership, Queen Juliana of the Netherlands. She pays no income tax—no tax, at least, on the official income that Parliament fixed for her in the year when she first came to the throne. But for this single vital factor of royal economics, the Civil List Act of 1952 would have been a disaster and, as things are, the Queen's financial advisers have cause for concern as they watch royal expenses repeatedly hurtling into the red under the upsurge of rising costs and unforeseen taxation. Alone among all the world's active professional women, indeed, Queen Elizabeth II has not had a pay rise for seventeen years and is not entitled to a salary increase for the rest of her life. All that glitters is definitely not gold these days at Buckingham Palace and, despite economies, it is widely recognised that the Queen is now continually drawing on her own private funds to help maintain the still impressive lustre of the British Crown.

The British government allows the Queen a total £475,000 a year, payable by quarterly warrants, and it has become dismayingly evident that this annual cash sum—the Civil List, as it is called—is no longer sufficient to cover the admittedly spectacular costs of maintaining the monarchy.

Even the British public, punch-drunk under successive financial crises, begin to realize the Queen herself needs a pay rise. We have recently seen the salaries of such figures as President Nixon and

Queen Juliana decisively doubled, while the Queen clearly loses out in her round-by-round fight against inflation. Those who write letters to the papers have pungently pointed out that her gross weekly salary would now be "sneered at by film stars and pop stars". With its huge circulation, the *Sunday Express* recently devoted much of its main page to the topic and scornfully demanded, "Has Britain sunk so low that it cannot pay the Sovereign the rate for the job?"

The Queen's financial circumstances, in any case, evidently justify a drastic review. It is two hundred years since King George III, overwrought and financially harassed, agreed to hand over the revenue of his royal lands in exchange for the fixed annuity of the Civil List. Successive monarchs renewed the arrangement and while the pound sterling embraced the most stable currency in the world the bargain was a fair one. Not long ago, however, a group of young lawyers, accountants and political economists of the Bow Group—an independent organisation of younger Conservatives—critically examined every modern cash fact of the monarchy and emerged with some remarkable findings. Parliament, they reported,* was "by no means lavish" in fixing the allowances for the Queen at the beginning of her reign.

The annual total of the Civil List looks like this:

Privy Purse (intended for all personal expenses)	£ 60,000
Salaries of Household	£185,000
Expenses of Household	£121,800
Royal Bounty (for charitable disbursements)	£ 13,200
Supplementary Provision	£ 95,000
	£475,000

To anyone except perhaps an accountant, these figures may appear astronomical . . . until you remember that they include the salaries of well over 200 people and the internal maintenance of six palaces. The Queen's father, George VI, in fact received £110,000 a

* An Evolving Monarchy, 1968.

year for *his* Privy Purse, back in the days before inflation when every pound or dollar would actually purchase thirty per cent more than it does at the present time. Even George V similarly received £110,000 for his personal spending money—and the widowed Queen Victoria was paid £60,000 in the affluent era when the pound sterling would purchase twelve times more than in 1969. It seems invidious that the Queen Regnant should still be paid this same sum today. In fact, the Queen receives £50,000 less a year in hard cash than the Privy Purse sum awarded her four predecessors; and, of course, this amounts to far less when measured in spending power. Although wages and prices have soared, Parliament provides the Queen with £31,000 less for household expenses than the £152,000 allowed her father during the austere years of war.

A still stranger point, which the Bow Group inquiry overlooked, is that twelve Commonwealth countries recognise Elizabeth as Queen but none have so far offered her a salary. Canada, Australia and New Zealand, for instance, pay her *nothing* in return for her royal duties and responsibilities . . . unless you tot up the occasional bills for hospitality or the value of the gifts presented to the Queen in the course of royal visits.

Just how poor *is* the Queen?

Most investigators begin by asking: how rich? They mistakenly assume that she personally owns, if not all her palaces, at least all the magnificent art treasures that furnish them. They argue that huge family fortunes must have been handed down through each generation, though no one has ever unearthed a single clue to the fabled real estate holdings that the Royal Family are supposed to own in downtown Manhattan and wishful scrutineers have disclosed no tangible pointer to any other royal hoard.

When comparisons were recently made, indeed, between the personal fortunes of Queen Elizabeth and Queen Juliana, the researchists readily turned up Juliana's extensive shareholdings in Anaconda Copper, KLM and Royal Dutch Shell . . . but ultimately assessed Queen Elizabeth's wealth chiefly by the £1,000,000 reputed value of her grandfather's historic stamp collection. Yet no one expects these precious 960 album pages ever to enter the auction room or become anything but a national possession.

Unsentimental financial persuasion could no more avail against the Queen's loyal sense of fitness than induce her to sell, say, her father's collection of jewelled cigarette-cases.

It's a cardinal error, also, to gross up the royal art collection—loosely estimated to be worth £50,000,000—as a ready reckoner to the Queen's personal fortune. It has been pointed out that a masterpiece by Rubens fetches £150,000 in the saleroom and that the Queen inherited at least five of his works. Over £140,000 has been paid at auction for a Gainsborough and the Queen possesses thirty. Paintings by Canaletto rate from £2,500 up and she "owns" fifty-three. A drawing by Leonardo da Vinci, not three inches square, fetched £19,000 at Sotheby's, but one cannot suppose that the Queen will exchange her 600 Leonardo drawings for perhaps £10,000,000 to establish a Royal Foundation of the Arts. Few of the pictures of the Crown art collection have been purchased personally by the Queen, and it appears that she could not sell one if she wished, except by an earth-shaking—and probably highly unconstitutional—Act of Parliament.

In acrid reality, the royal pictures are as inalienable as the Crown Jewels and must be passed on to the successors to the Crown. Everything is entailed, as the lawyers say, held for future heirs rather than the immediate possessor. And since the royal art treasures have cost about £300,000 in the past seventeen years merely to maintain for posterity, some might regard them as more a personal liability than an asset.

To briefly cast over the Queen's more personal wealth, she owns the royal estates of Balmoral and Sandringham, purchased in Queen Victoria's day, but none of her other palaces. She could in theory part with any one of her 900 items of personal jewellery, including such treasures as the £46,000 pink diamond brooch—gallantly presented to her by Quebec-born John Thorburn Williamson—which she wore for her 1968 Christmas TV film. The Queen has a life interest in the profits of Ascot racecourse—although she ploughs them all back—and in the revenues of the Duchy of Lancaster. But my close study of these possessions does not lead to an over-all picture of readily saleable or realisable riches.

Few people are aware, for instance, that the Queen's father, King

George VI, had to acquire the private royal estates of Balmoral and Sandringham direct from the Duke of Windsor at the time of the Abdication, presumably for a heavy cash consideration. According to the knowledgeable Lord Beaverbrook, the ex-monarch departed into exile with more than £850,000, inevitably inflicting a sharp clip of his brother's investment income which must impoverish the Queen to this day.

Mr William Ellis, former superintendant of Windsor Castle, has told of his astonishment one day when the Queen flicked through a bundle of chintz curtain patterns and said regretfully, "We shall just have to find something cheaper." The redecoration of two rooms at the Castle had been discussed, but the Queen changed her mind and confessed, "We had better only do one this year because of expense."

When the shocked Mr Ellis noticed that threadbare carpets were patched with canvas underneath to give them extra years of wear, he perhaps failed to realise that Her Majesty was merely attempting to balance her *official* budget. Even when she burns logs from Windsor Great Park on the Castle hearths, she is technically liable to pay for the fuel. The broad rule has been laid down that the government is responsible for the structure of her official residences, and the Queen for the maintenance of the contents. The ballroom at Buckingham Palace was recently regilded at government expense but the Queen had to pay for cleaning the six chandeliers.

Outside Buckingham Palace, the innermost secrets of Elizabeth's private income are probably known only to two or three trusted officials of the firm of Coutts and Co., the royal bankers. So steeped in formality that the male clerks still wear elegant frockcoats and must be clean-shaven, Coutts' have supervised the ebb and flow of royal funds for over two centuries with complete integrity and discretion.

Before they took over the royal account, Queen Anne netted only £6,000 a year from all her landed wealth. Coutts, however, helped George III to accumulate sizeable deposits, only to see the cash lavished on the palace-building extravagances of his son, George IV. The young Queen Victoria thus inherited little, but Coutts hoarded millions for her in widowhood . . . only once more to see almost the entire fortune dispersed early this century in legacies to her innumerable descendants all over Europe. Since Edward VII was provided for, and was never in his mother's favour, he probably received little except Balmoral, and so the fortunes of the royal house were no doubt again reduced to low ebb.

The contents of royal wills are never published, but it has been claimed that Queen Mary left £380,000 nett only after Coutts' experts had shrewdly channelled her spare finances into a family trust fund. Her estate nevertheless had to find thousands in death duties, a tax from which the Sovereign alone is exempt. More recently, when the Princess Royal died suddenly and left assets of £328,000, the head of Coutts as an executor of her will probably advised her son, Lord Harewood, in realising investments and selling antiques and jewells to pay £158,000 to the tax collector.

In a bygone, more scandalous era, old Thomas Coutts lived over his office in the Strand, having been happily married for years to his brother's former maid-servant. At the age of 80, four days after his wife's funeral, he married a thirty-eight-year-old actress, whose heiress, Baroness Burdett-Coutts, was similarly wed at sixty-seven to a young American of twenty-eight. Today's chairman of the firm, Mr Seymour Egerton, remains however a bachelor, though irreproachably linked with ten of the top families of the British aristocracy. One of his co-directors is brother of the Countess of Euston, who is lady in waiting to the Queen, and a former director now retired, is none other than the Queen Mother's nephew, Lord Granville.

When the Queen goes to her bank, once every six or seven years, she is entertained to lunch in a directors' luncheon room adorned with family portraits. The boardroom, too, is decorated with a Chinese wallpaper older and finer than any in Buckingham Palace. And on the rare occasions when she cashes a personal cheque—except for the crown-and-cipher her white-and-grey cheques are like any other—the transaction is naturally as private as that of any other client and perhaps somewhat more so.

The Coutts passbooks, on the other hand, provided the Queen's accountants with useful evidence when parliament staged its last big inquiry into royal finance back in 1952. George VI, it was disclosed, habitually dipped into his personal cash to meet the expense of being a king. In the last two years of his life, he contributed £90,000 of his own funds towards Household salaries and expenses, and in five years he had conscientiously overspent in this way by nearly half a million.

Apart from Coutts, the Queen's similar over-spending is probably known only to her Treasurer, Lord Tryon, who began his finance-wise career as an A.D.C. to the Governor-General of Canada. And in handling and observing the provisions of the £475,000 Civil List, his own toughest problem is undoubtedly the sum of £95,000 allocated to "Supplementary Provision".

Parliament, in its wisdom, intended this partly as a contingency sum, allowing *twenty* per cent for future inflation, and partly as a provision for expenses of other unpaid members of the Royal Family. In reality, the rate of inflation has been *forty* per cent above 1952 values and the Supplement cannot begin to take care of expenses at today's level for such active and duty-conscious royalties as Princess Alexandra and the Duke of Kent.

Lord Tryon administers the Queen's official Privy Purse income of £60,000. After he has paid the Queen's dress bills and disbursed for her handbags and hats . . . and after he has cleared the schooling of Prince Andrew and Prince Edward and met Princess Anne's expenses, there is obviously plenty in hand. Yet the balance becomes startlingly less when the Queen undertakes an overseas tour involving the charter of planes or trains. It has now become a point of economy to use the royal yacht *Britannia*—paid for by the Ministry of Defence—whenever possible.

The lack of travel allowances for the Queen rates as one of the more glaring omissions of the royal budget as reflected in the Civil List. The Bow Group investigators also assert that the Civil List sum of £185,000 for salaries of the Royal Household is probably exceeded "by a substantial margin". The Queen's close personal staff, such as the Private Secretary, Sir Martin Charteris, are men of top executive status who would be underpaid at £7,500 a year. Their salaries have never been made known, but in 1962 evidence was given in Parliament that the average individual cost of soldiers used as supplementary servants was £970 a year. The Civil Service Union reveals that it numbers 200 of the Queen's domestic or industrial staff among its members, from Windsor linen maids to Scottish night watchman at Holyroodhouse. The Westminster voters' lists also indicate that Buckingham Palace has over 100 people "living in", ranging from chauffeurs and chefs to administrative officials. If the Parliamentary £970 a year applies to only two hundred people at today's price levels, the resulting £194,000 considerably exceeds the Queen's overall £185,000 allowance for all annual salaries.

Some of the Palace staff are on daily transfer to Windsor Castle but the Queen equally has to pay maintenance salaries for St James's Palace and Holyroodhouse, Kensington Palace and part of Hampton Court, where she gives rent-free "grace-and-favour" apartments to a number of pensioned widows of former national heroes. Scores of ceremonial members of the Royal Household—of the calibre of the Lord Steward and the Master of the Horse—exact no salary and, apart from principals, the office work of state is probably managed by not more that thirty people in the £2,000 a year class. But one can see where the money goes.

The two hundred "royal members" of the Civil Service Union received a pay rise not long ago after negotiations through the Ministry of Labour. For a bookbinder in the royal archives, the agreed increase meant £1 a week. Daily cleaners drew £50 or so in back-dated pay.

Unlike a business enterprise, the Queen cannot however offset rising costs by increasing her revenue. She has elected to pay an employer's share of social security contributions for her staff, as well as personal pensions on a wide scale. An entirely unforeseen and far sterner strain upon her resources arose, however, in 1966 when the Government instituted the Selective Employment Tax, designed to transfer manpower from all forms of service to manufacturing or export jobs. The idea, as one wit put it, was that Palace housemaids should can beans in Birmingham. In effect, the tax has to be paid by employers on every employee, with a compensating refund according to export and industrial values, but the Queen has not been cast for this purpose in the repayment category of whaling, car hire or open-cast mining. At an average 48s. weekly for every man and 24s. for each woman in royal employ, the Queen probably pays at least £20,000 S.E.T. a year—and has not yet elected to challenge the Whitehall decision that she should do so.

The Queen's £121,800 for Household expenses similarly goes into the red in "heating and eating". The Queen meets the cost of State Banquets and other diplomatic entertainments and, as hostess to the Commonwealth, she has to stage three or four garden parties every summer, often for as many as 7,000 guests at a time (at 10s. a head). She even pays for the upkeep of Queen Victoria's tomb—and faces rising prices for everything from silver polish and carpet-cleaning to the £25 cost of a new Royal Standard when her personal flag gets torn apart by wind and weather.

Experts from the lush Savoy and Claridge's hotel group, and accountants such as Sir Basil Smallpeice of BOAC and Cunard—now the Queen's Administrative Adviser—have all attempted to prune royal costings, without significant change. Little was saved, for example, when the Queen discontinued paying £1 a head royal bounty for triplets. In practice, most parents had long since preferred to frame the royal cheque rather than cash it. But the Queen's £13,200 bounty fund scarcely begins to cover her charity subscriptions and donations ... or minor disbursements like the sixty £2 Christmas puddings that she gives her Palace policemen.

Tended by one of her paid chaplains, a former schoolmaster-parson with a two-room Palace office suite, the Royal Almonry remains the least publicised of royal departments. Apart from the traditional Maundy Money for old folk, gifts for innumerable good causes are set afloat in a continuous current of stealthy philanthropy.

Distorted by seventeen years of inflation, the Queen's Civil List allowances are indeed drastically out of date. There remains the unpalatable fact that the figures were fixed in 1952 for her lifetime, and she cannot herself renounce the arrangement or go back on the bargain, even if the financial changes of the next forty years reduce her to penury. If she could restore the status quo and claim the income of the Crown Lands that are still legally hers, she would in fact be six or seven times better off.

It is well known that, in exchange for the Civil List, the Queen followed the patten of George III and turned over to the government the revenues, mainly in rents, of the former Crown Lands. This lucrative slice of real estate now includes huge areas of central London and agricultural possessions ranging over nearly 400,000 acres.

Highly trained men of business, the Crown Estates Commissioners in 1968 bumped up the rents of jostling Carnaby Street, dredged the offshore seabed of the English Channel for mineral wealth and paid £3,725,000 profit into the national exchequer. Such an inflow tends to make the average Briton philosophic about the rising costs of royalty . . . and makes the Queen's £475,000 seem all the more meagre.

It looks as if the British-style monarchy is still the world's best buy in constitutional government. President Nixon gets $200,000 a year taxable, plus $50,000 "to assist in defraying expenses" but White House overheads amounting to $2,000,000 are met under other appropriations. Even the simplified style of Scandinavian monarchy seems fairly expensive. King Gustav of Sweden draws as much as £220,000 from an eight million population, together with £47,000 for firewood and coal, £30,000 for the upkeep of furniture and the considerable sum of £134,000 for the "police, lighting and cleaning and fire precautions of the royal palaces," a grand rather than simple total of £431,000. King Frederik of Denmark draws £285,000 annually from his five million people. The sum is subject to an increase based on the cost of living and in fact zoomed by £66,000 between 1965 and 1968. King Baudouin actually nets over £484,000 from only ten million subjects. When Queen Juliana of the Netherlands complained that she could no longer maintain her royal dignity, palaces and servants on an overall official income of £250,000, the Dutch parliament nearly doubled her pay to £520,000 tax-free.

Queen Elizabeth II pays no tax on her Civil List but obeys a distant law of 1862 decreeing that she should pay income tax on her *private* income. If from all private investment sources she draws as much as £100,000 a year, she pays about £86,000 tax. This, of course, is the drastic rate for any British citizen in this tax bracket. By her own agreement in 1952, moreover, the Queen has been returning most of the income of the Duchy of Cornwall to the government "to help reduce the cost of the Civil List". It appeared that the revenues lay within the Queen's disposal during Prince Charles's minority.

In contrast, Queen Victoria and Prince Albert in their day hoarded the money until it reached a nest-egg of £660,000 on their eldest son's coming-of-age. One third of this was used for the private purchase of Sandringham. The modern revenues of the Duchy of Cornwall have, however, been running at £201,000 a year on rents from 140,000 acres of farmland and moor, profits from oyster beds and a useful pocket of real estate in London. During his minority, only £10,000 taxable—about £4,000 net—was set aside for Prince Charles. At eighteen he began drawing £30,000 gross per annum. On his twenty-first birthday in November, 1969, he becomes master of the entire Duchy income, but it seems unlikely that he will retain more than £25,000 a year after tax.

By comparison the government annuities paid to other members of the Royal Family are completely straightforward: £70,000 to the Queen Mother, £40,000 to the Duke of Edinburgh, £35,000 to the Duke of Gloucester, £15,000 to Princess Margaret, £6,000 to Princess Anne at twenty-one, all taxable after the royal secretaries have produced certified expense accounts.

Not that inquisitive citizens need imagine that the Queen is crying all the way to the bank. When her chief accountant, Mr Henry Pinnock, has underlined the deficit on her official budget, she is still an extremely rich woman in her own right, although the chief source of her wealth is little-known and rarely publicised.

A clue can be found in one of London's curious old customs. A City lawyer once a year scrupulously weighs six horseshoes and sixty-one nails as a quit-rent for the site of a blacksmith's forge in the Strand. The forge has vanished but the rent has been paid for the past 600 years, a symbol of the origin of more sensibly economic ground-rents that the Queen is believed to draw from the Savoy Hotel and the Savoy Theatre, home of Gilbert and Sullivan, as well as from the shops of the Strand and modern office blocks nearby in Aldwych. In the neighbouring Chapel of the Savoy, the choir sing "God Save the Queen . . . bless our noble Duke" and by this they mean, not Prince Philip, but the Queen herself in her unique role as Duke of Lancaster. In 1359, John o'Gaunt, fourth son of Edward III, married Blanche, the heiress to the Duchy of Lancaster, and so gained the nucleus of an estate destined to grow to 52,000 acres. His son, King Henry IV, succeeded as Duke of Lancaster and the holding has been regarded as the personal possession of the Sovereign ever since.

By a neat and perhaps astute oversight, it escaped being thrown into George III's bargain over the Crown estates. By a still neater fiction, as a possession inextricably interwoven with the Crown, its revenues are exempt from income tax and death duties and currently yield £160,000 a year. Apart from the London estates, it includes most of the spa of Harrogate as well as industrial regions of Yorkshire and Lancashire and various picturesque perquisites. If anyone in the Duchy dies without traceable heirs, the money goes by ancient custom to the Duke, i.e. the Queen.

Some years ago the Inland Revenue authorities attempted to tax the profits of some re-opened Derbyshire lead mines. On discovering, however, that the receipts went to the Duchy of Lancaster, they had to withdraw. The Queen in fact nets £24,000 in dividends from investments, most of the remaining revenue being in rents.

The Duchy must be passed inalienably to her heirs and cannot be sold off, but the House of Commons is supposed to have borne the revenues in mind when they agreed on their unelastic Civil List. If the Queen is in fact spending £100,000 Duchy cash in maintaining the monarchy, she will be left with £60,000, although some experts believe that the real margin is already very much less.

The Queen spends part of her spare cash on Balmoral and on her racing activities. Her private Scottish home was bought for £31,500 in 1852—the year, as it happened, when an eccentric miser named Nield left Queen Victoria a useful legacy of £250,000—but does not pay for itself in either the shooting or forestry. Sandringham, the Queen's other private home, may be entailed for the Prince of Wales, and Prince Philip is credited with making it a self-supporting sporting and agricultural estate. Yet, above all, Sandringham is pleasantly subsidised by Aureole, the Queen's wonder racehorse, standing at stud and yielding from his bookings some £16,000 a year.

In the first ten years of her reign, as we have seen elsewhere, the Queen had fantastic racing luck, winning over £150,000 in prize money. In seven recent years she has grossed £85,000, roughly equalising after paying training and stable expenses. Here again, as with Ascot racecourse, which she has equipped with £1,000,000 worth of new grandstands, any profits are ploughed back.

Little of the Queen's wealth can thus be visualised as take-away money. There's little ready cash in the royal kitty and if the Queen continues to subsidise the institution of royalty from her private income, the bottom of the royal coffers may be scraped faster than most people suppose.

It seems unlikely that the Queen will ever press for a pay rise. As a young woman, at her glittering Coronation, she stood for a time in a simple white shift, a symbol that in the essence of royal dedication she stripped herself of earthly riches. And Queen Elizabeth II is a woman of the highest ideals who continually evinces a determination never to make a personal profit by reigning over us.